European Monetary Union and Exchange Rate Dynamics

Springer-Verlag Berlin Heidelberg GmbH

Paul J. J. Welfens

European Monetary Union and Exchange Rate Dynamics

New Approaches and Application to the Euro

With 26 Figures
and 12 Tables

Springer

Prof. Dr. Paul J. J. Welfens
University of Potsdam
European Institute for International
Economic Relations (EIIW)
August-Bebel-Str. 89
14489 Potsdam
Germany
http://www.euroeiiw.de

ISBN 978-3-642-63228-0

Library of Congress Cataloging-in-Publication Data applied for
Die Deutsche Bibliothek – CIP-Einheitsaufnahme
Welfens, Paul J. J.: European Monetary Union and Exchange Rate Dynamics: New Approaches and Application to the Euro; with 12 tables / Paul J. J. Welfens. – Berlin; Heidelberg; New York; Barcelona; Hong Kong; London; Milan; Paris; Singapore; Tokyo: Springer, 2001
ISBN 978-3-642-63228-0 ISBN 978-3-642-56913-5 (eBook)
DOI 10.1007/978-3-642-56913-5

Originally published by Springer-Verlag Berlin · Heidelberg 2001
Softcover reprint of the hardcover 1st edition 2001

Hardcover-Design: Erich Kirchner, Heidelberg

SPIN 10733702 43/2202-5 4 3 2 1 0 – Printed on acid-free paper

Preface

The creation of the European System of Central Banks (ESCB) and the start of the Euro in 1999 are historical marks for Europe. With the start of the new currency and the ECB the world economy also is facing a major structural change and new challenges. In a historical perspective the European Monetary Union has the unique feature that a common new institution, the ECB, has been created. This is in marked contrast to the Scandinavian and the Latin Monetary Union (France, Italy, Belgium and Switzerland) in the late 19th century which was a period in which national central banks were created in order to stabilize the respective national financial systems. In the starting year 1999 the European Central Bank had favorable conditions in the sense that low inflation rates and an economic upswing had coincided; while this should contribute to a Euro appreciation in the long run the short term exchange rate developments were in marked contrast as the new currency lost about 1/5 of its value within 16 months; while exchange rate volatility has not been unusual in the 1980s the continued and strong fall of the Euro vis-à-vis the US dollar, the pound, the Swiss franc and the Yen has raised concerns. The strong initial fall of the Euro has created some problems in establishing the new currency as a strong contender for the US dollar. Moreover, there are some theoretical challenges since the portfolio model offers a rather different message than the purchasing power parity.

For the EU there will be the challenge of proving that the new system has economic and political advantages that make monetary integration sustainable, moreover, the Community has to define its new role in the global monetary system at the end of the 1990s. The start of the 21st century certainly sees the USA as the world's leading financial center and the dollar as the world's dominant currency, but this position is now challenged by the newcomer Euro and Euroland provided that the EU (Euroland) can maintain low inflation and achieve considerable economic growth. Creation of the Euro itself should stimulate economic growth in the medium term in Euroland since the new currency reinforces price transparency and competition on the one hand, on the other hand, it stimulates restructuring in large firms and facilitates creation of new companies as a consequence of financial market integration. Japan, which played a major role as a challenger in the 1980s, has come under pressure in the wake of a deep political and economic crisis in the 1990s. However, Japan's main problem at the beginning of the 21st century is its declining innovativeness – declining growth rates in international patents stand for a structural supply side weakness. By contrast, Euroland´s innovation record has improved.

Not all EU countries are members of Euroland. However, with 11 countries starting on January 1999 and the creation of a joint central bank in Euroland, the ESCB, a historical step has been made for Western Europe but possibly also for other regions in the world economy. Economic integration and political cooperation can, under certain circumstances, lead to a situation in which countries give up monetary sovereignty in order to more easily achieve prosperity and stability. Prior to the start of the Euro, politicians agreed on convergence requirements – concerning price stability (plus interest rate convergence) and fiscal criteria plus the political independence of the national central bank – so that special side-constraints were imposed for monetary union. From a theoretical point of view it is somewhat doubtful that the criteria chosen are really adequate, but they are defendable to some extent. In chapter I the analysis shows how difficult the convergence process was in the EU and which major benefits one can expect from monetary union. We also analyze the diversity of EU countries and highlight some basic aspects of the monetary transmission process – the analysis necessarily includes some issues of labor market policies, which are controversial in the EU. The focus of the analysis on specific issues of the convergence process and of basic theoretical and empirical issues in the context of the New Europe; indeed, the EU has started monetary union at a moment when the eastern EU enlargement already is under negotiation. For the EU-15 there are risks from international financial markets as well as from the economic opening up to eastern Europe whose considerable growth – mainly in the Visegrad countries – is welcome by the EU. However, one should not overlook that diverse economic structures and trade orientations of EU countries imply divergent exposure to potential shocks, which is important for the convergence issue.

Chapter II is almost purely theoretical. We look into the BRANSON portfolio model and modify this model by taking into account some standard arguments from the TOBIN portfolio analysis. Furthermore we link this to the production function and the goods market (modified MUNDELL-FLEMING model). Moreover, we link the modified portfolio model with a new model setup for the goods markets; and we present new theoretical and empirical results.

Chapter III is about exchange rate regimes and exchange rate policy issues. The start of the Euro has caused a lively debate concerning the need for a new Bretton Woods System in Europe and elsewhere. However, there is no strong case for a new Bretton Woods System – while one can state many arguments for more transparency and strict supervision of financial markets. The analysis has a focus both on trade, foreign direct investment and issues of global or regional crisis management. We also analyze some issues of EMS II and of the currency band debate. Finally, some selected aspects of exchange rate regimes of transforming countries in eastern Europe are discussed.

While the start of the Euro has many aspects we have focussed only on selected ones, but one may hope that some of the most important ones have been addressed. As regards theoretical innovations future research should include broad empirical analysis. I hope that the study presented encourages a wide-ranging debate about exchange rate regimes and exchange rate dynamics. I am grateful to

DG II, European Commission, which offered a stimulating research environment in early 1998. Finally I would like to express my gratitude to Ina Brüggemann, Juliane Kinsele, Karl Hummel, Tim Yarling, Andre Jungmittag and Ralf Wiegert for their editorial support.

Potsdam and Washington, July 2000

Paul J.J. Welfens, Jean Monnet Professor in European Economic Integration

Table of Contents

A. European Monetary Union: Start of the Euro and the Need for Complementary Measures in Euroland

1. Introduction

Monetary union will create a new monetary regime in "Euroland" and could affect public deficits, investment, growth and employment in a positive way in the medium and long term. However, one should distinguish between short-term and medium-term transition problems which could include rising unemployment in some countries and long-term opportunities related to employment, economic growth and wealth effects. Whether such opportunities really can be realized is likely to depend on national economic policy behavior, collective bargaining adjustments and policy coordination in Euroland. This analysis will focus on some of the main issues.

The steep fall of the Euro in 1999/2000 has raised concerns about the viability of EMU. While many critics have argued that the Euro would be more inflationary than traditionally stable European currencies – e.g. DM, Guilder, Austrian Shilling or FF (in the 1990s) – the first real challenge of the EMU project has come from the external side: The strong appreciation of the US dollar, the British Pound and the Yen has raised critical questions about monetary union and the options of economic policy in Euroland. Having decided in favor of a long three year transition for switching from Euro deposits to introducing Euro coins and notes the starting group of the Euro has taken unnecessary risks as the long transition could – faced temporarily by massive expected devaluations – even lead to speculative attacks against the Euro and a shaken political will in some countries to support the move towards the new currency.

While the dollar is supported by a clearly designed political US system – with the minister of finance and the president of the Federal Reserve System cooperating visibly – the political system of Euroland has unclear structures. It consists of 11 countries with 11 ministers of finance who loosely cooperate in the Euro-11 group, which is a subsystem of the ECOFIN. The international public will always notice divergences among the 11 ministers of finance who have failed to agree on a system under which only one minister would speak on Euro matters – lack of political integration in Euroland is a potential problem here (more cooperation might, however, have other unpleasant drawbacks, e.g. reinforcing resistance against national deregulation/reregulation). Moreover, the ECB which together with the 11 national central banks of the Euro starter countries forms the European System of Central Banks (ESCB) is also not free of friction. As national central banks continue to publish their respective analysis of the economic situation there is ample room for divergent views, e.g. the Deutsche Bundesbank publishing analytical statements in its monthly reports that contradict those of the European Central Bank. Contrasting views of "regional central banks" and the ECB would be less of a problem if the monthly reports of the regional central banks came under the clear heading of research reports, that is there would no longer be a mix of research and implicit policy statements. For the international public the present system would look even more confusing as more EU countries join the Euro area in the future.

Start of the Euro

The Euro group of eleven countries has started in 1999 with a remarkable inflation convergence where the convergence requirement for the Euro starter group was based on the three best-performing countries with an identical inflation rate of 1.2% in 1997, namely Ireland, France and Austria (1.2%, 1.2% and 1.1%, respectively). Disregarding Greece the EU countries were in the range of 1.1 to 1.9% in 1997 and are likely to achieve similar figures in 1999/2000. As much as the strong disinflation record of EU countries in 1993-98 contributed to rising unemployment, one may expect that stable low inflation rates will improve prospects of employment growth. The costs of disinflation which typically include rising unemployment rates have leveled, and no further significant increase of unemployment should occur as expected and actual inflation rates have converged at a very low level. This does not rule out transitory spurs of rising unemployment as a rising number of firms – facing sharper price competition after 1999 in Euroland – engage in cross-border mergers & acquisitions; such M&As in Euroland could go along with lay-offs in the newly merged companies. Moreover, there are some risks related to issues of asymmetric shocks which – given the absence of the exchange rate instrument – could cause rising unemployment and other problems in Euroland. It also will be important to get the outsiders on board within a reasonable time frame, where the UK, given the significance of its financial market, is the most important case. Among the criticism against EMU the argument was prominent that Euroland was likely to face asymmetric shocks which would require national exchange rate adjustment which in monetary union would no longer be possible. While this argument cannot be dismissed on a priori grounds one has to raise the question to which extent disturbances in the period of European Monetary System I (1979-98) were mainly monetary in nature. With the creation of the European Central Bank and the Euro, respectively, monetary shocks from within the EU could be relatively unimportant. Moreover, monetary union will change market structures and certaintly reinforce intra-Euroland trade so that criticism based on correlations of past shocks is rather doubtful (BOFINGER, 1994; FRANKEL/ROSE, 1996). Changes in market structures stemming from the introduction of the Euro – above all the increase in intra-Euroland trade – might indeed support the case of a monetary union in the EU (BLACK, 1997).

Labor market rigidity has been a problem for many years in continental EU countries. Some of these rigidities might be removed as a consequence of more competition pressure in Euroland which will no longer allow trade unions to uphold barriers erected in defense of rents by entrenched labor unions at the expense of unemployed workers (SAINT-PAUL, 1996). To the extent that monetary union alters the balance of power and stimulates policymakers to help remove labor market rigidities, improved prospects for more labor market flexibility could contribute to employment creation. However, trade unions in various countries of Euroland will also tend to cooperate more intensively – a process which, given the differences of per capita income and organization modes across EU countries, is likely to take many years.

Monetary union is largely a political decision where the selection criteria have not been based in a straightforward manner on the theory of optimum currency area which has been discussed in the literature (e.g. FRATIANNI/VON HAGEN, 1992; DE GRAUWE, 1994; SIEBERT, 1996; WELFENS, 1996, 1997; FRANKEL/ROSE, 1996; KENEN, 1995) but rather on pragmatically chosen convergence criteria. Unemployment rates were not included in the catalogue of criteria, not least because the economics profession largely subscribes to a vertical long-term Phillips curve. However, it is clear that high sustained EU unemployment rates would undermine the success of a monetary union with price stability – if only for the reason that political parties could claim that budgetary discipline and low inflation rates are the ultimate culprit for high unemployment. From an economist's point of view a crucial question thus is to solve the unemployment problem within monetary union and to identify adequate complementary measures that contribute to a sustainable low inflation monetary union in Europe. Low long-term inflation rates also mean low nominal interest rates and therefore a higher EU money demand and hence more positive welfare effects than before.

Given the high unemployment rate of about 11% in continental EU countries in 1997 and 10% in 1998/99 future progress in raising employment will be extremely important. While direct employment effects of EMU are likely to be limited, thus leaving the Community at an unemployment rate of roughly 10% (with relatively low figures of 5% and 7.2% in the pre-ins Denmark and the UK; Sweden has around 9%); besides Luxembourg with 3.5%, only Austria and the Netherlands recorded a low rate of around 5% in late 1998/99 - equivalent to the US rate of 4.5%. As is well known a major problem in Euroland is not just the unemployment figure but the high share of long-term unemployment (unemployed for more than one year) which is close to 40% of all unemployed while the US figure is only 10%. A favorable unemployment record in Denmark, the UK and somewhat less so in Sweden and Greece has led to favorable budget positions – on average a surplus – for Euro outsiders in 1998/99.

Since firms in the fully integrated post-1999 EU single market will face new incentives to rationalize their operations and to fully exploit economies of scale, one may expect only modest direct positive investment and employment effects from the creation of EMU. Indeed a crucial issue concerning EMU will be trade creation effects on the one hand, and, on the other hand, effects in the nontradables sector – with an uncertain effect on overall employment and economic welfare (section 2). Regarding investment under the new EMU regime we want to analyze the prospects for investment growth both in the medium term defined by the transition towards full price arbitrage in Euroland and the introduction of Euro coins and bills in 2002 (section 3). The monetary transmission mechanism in Euroland is likely to differ across member countries, but it also could be different relative to the EMS-I period (section 4). Relatively low investment in machinery and equipment in EU countries is partly attributable to an insufficient number of new firms created; dynamic new firms in the US which are in the age bracket of five to ten years account for a considerable share of overall investment as well as for a high share of product and process innovations which are crucial for employment growth and international competitiveness. We therefore raise the issue of underdeveloped and partly inefficient EU capital markets (section 5). Section 6 takes a closer look at relative price changes and real convergence in Euroland. Furthermore, one has to ask which reform elements are necessary in the EU to combat high unemployment figures in most Euro countries. Part of the relevant analysis clearly will concern labor market reforms to the extent that greater wage dispersion, higher wage flexibility and increased labor mobility are needed in monetary union. Since labor mobility in the EU is lower than in the US on the one hand, and, on the other hand has declined over the past decades, it will be important to identify the reasons for low labor mobility and policy options to increase mobility (section 7). Section 8 briefly discusses the implications of the previous sections for the problem of budgetary consolidation, and section 9 deals with potential EU protectionism. Section 10 raises some questions with respect to long term real exchange rate developments. Finally, we offer a summary and some conclusions. At the bottom line we find that a prudent monetary policy of interest rate reductions should be combined with growth-enhancing fiscal and structural policies, more differentiated wage policies and other innovations in economic policy.

2. The Single Market, Growth Perspectives and Welfare Effects of the Euro

Monetary union will reinforce price transparency and reduce transaction costs in trade among countries of Euroland. From a theoretical point of view this is equivalent to reducing tariffs; i.e. one can expect trade creation and trade diversion effects. Trade creation concerns the rising trade among Euro-partners, while trade diversion could occur both vis-à-vis EU outsiders and non-EU countries. A priori the net welfare effect is uncertain, but it is well-known that trade creation effects will dominate if monetary union stimulates growth in Euroland sufficiently. Since the introduction of the Euro has pro-competitive effects one may indeed expect that there will be a rise of the economic growth rate and one-off real income gains. Whether Euroland's economic growth will really benefit from the Euro will mainly depend on five effects (WELFENS, 2000):

- Increasing cross-border M&As which could raise factor productivity but also might raise unemployment and create additional uncertainty among workers which in turn could impair growth of consumption. Increasing M&As will raise the price of existing capital (P^K), Tobin's q defined as P^K/P – where P stands for the price of new capital and output, respectively – will exceed one so that there is an incentive to invest in new capital and equipment, respectively.
- Falling costs of capital as more transparent and competitive bonds markets will contribute to reduced nominal and real interest rates which in turn should stimulate stock markets (with secondary expansionary consumption effects).
- To the extent that the creation of the Euro stimulates capital inflows – in particular foreign direct investment inflows – the investment-output ratio I/Y will increase which will raise output growth. This development could be reinforced by a more competitive capital market in Euroland which brings about a more efficient filter process with respect to the selection of investment projects, that is the marginal product of capital (Y_K) will increase. This holds since output growth $g_Y = (I/Y)\ Y_K$.
- From a Schumpeterian perspective it is not simply the average profit rate which will determine investment growth in Euroland (the traditional reasoning argues that a high profit rate will stimulate investment), rather high inter-firm and inter-sectoral profit rate differentials which signal extra profit opportunities in some sectors and firms will go along with high investment growth.
- The expansion of the stock of money and of the stock of bonds: From a portfolio-theoretical perspective a conservative monetary policy of the ECB in combination with reduction of debt-GDP ratio ((B/P)/Y) will impair economic growth with respect to risk aspects real financial wealth (M/P+B/P) where real capital K is complementary. With the stock of real financial wealth declining – at least relative to real output Y – relative demand for real capital will fall; here we see negative effects of a short-term oriented strategy of achieving the debt-GDP Maastricht target ratio of 60% in some countries; restrictive monetary policy in combination with a declining debt-GDP ratio implies that the price of existing capital should fall relative to investment goods so that investment demand is reduced which in turn impairs output growth. Even if the combination of restrictive monetary policy and budget consolidation in Euroland did not directly contribute to depressed investment demand in Euroland's core countries Germany, France and Italy, one should not overlook the problem that monetary union in a global setting with a rising role of foreign direct investment (FDI) raises crucial challenges: If capital abroad K* - from a

Euroland perspective this de facto means the US - and domestic capital K are substitutes, there is the risk that relatively improving earnings on real capital abroad will translate a rising demand for existing capital into high FDI outflows from Euroland. The demand for existing real capital in the US will increase which will go along with a stock market boom and later by high investment demand as new capital goods have become relatively cheap compared to existing capital equipment. Since 1997 the US growth rate has exceeded that of Euroland by more than 1.5 percentage points and that of Japan by more than 3 percentage points (see Fig. A1).

Fig. A1: Growth Rates in the US, Japan and Euroland 1994-99

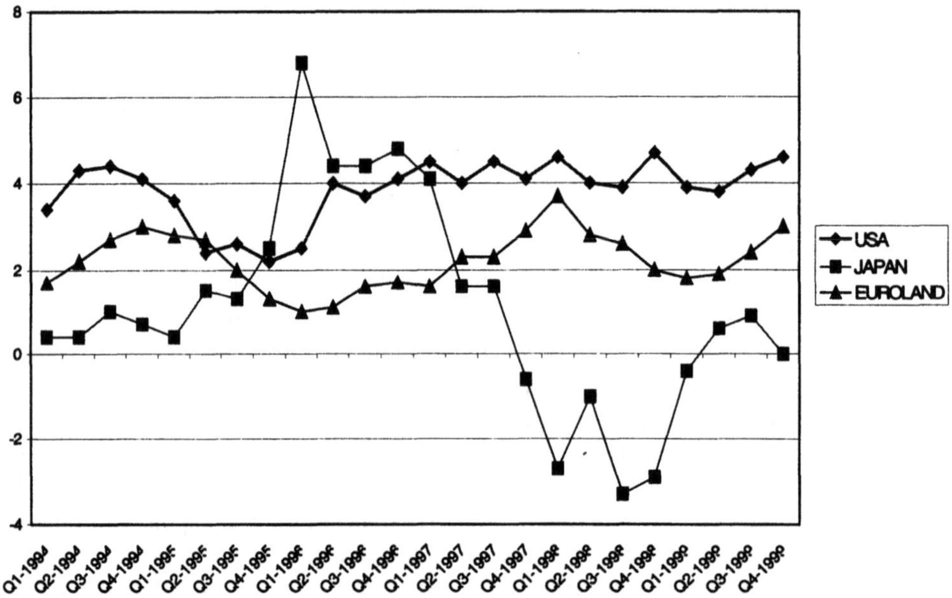

Source: ECB (2000), Monthly Bulletin, May 2000.

Long Term Welfare Effects

Some important permanent gains from the Euro are for former high inflation countries, namely positive long term economic welfare effects from the downward inflation convergence. According to traditional analysis the welfare loss H – relative to output Y – from inflation can be calculated in terms of the real interest rate r, the inflation rate π and the interest elasticity (ε) of the real money demand

(m) as follows: $H/Y = (r + 0.5\ \pi)\ \varepsilon\ (m/Y)$. With an inflation rate of 10%, a real interest rate of 4% and an absolute number of 0.05 for the elasticity, a ratio of $m/Y= 0.5$ will lead to a welfare loss of ¼ % of output. To put it differently, the welfare gain of a switch from an inflation rate of 10% to price stability under a new monetary regime is ¼ % of gross domestic product. This does not sound impressive; however, capitalized at a 4% real interest rate for an infinite time horizon the present discounted value of the new regime is indeed equivalent to one year's output. This positive wealth effect indeed has to be taken into account in an adequate portfolio approach of exchange rate determination; the new monetary regime amounts to an increase of the stock of wealth. One should, however, not overlook that disinflation in Italy and other EU countries has raised unemployment and reduced growth temporarily, that is long term Eurobenefits can only be achieved at short term costs.

In addition to traditional analysis one may point to the inflation tax which indeed should be partially considered as a welfare loss. This holds to the extent that "spending efficiency" in the private sector is higher than in the government sector. With a rising inflation tax rising government spending will be crowding out private expenditures that would be associated with lower costs and higher productivity, respectively. If the differential in productivities is h, the additional welfare cost of inflation is $hm\pi$, or – relative to output – $hm\pi/Y$. With $m/Y=0.5$, an inflation rate of 10%, and a productivity differential of 20% the negative welfare effect of inflation is 1% of gross domestic product. In this new perspective the economic burden of inflation seems to be much higher than the traditional analysis would suggest.

The welfare cost of inflation will increase if the interest elasticity of the demand for money would rise. In the literature (ROTHER, 1997) one can find arguments both for the case that monetary union will raise the interest elasticity and that the Euro will reduce it. This therefore is an empirical issue.

In a dynamic perspective the Euro will increase allocative efficiency since its introduction has pro-competitive effects. To the extent that this stimulates a rise in (cross-border) M&As there will be job losses in the early Euro period, but there should be positive long-term growth and employment effects which are partly reflecting positive welfare and income effects similar to those known from textbook models of trade liberalization. Moreover, rising FDI flows within Euroland should raise efficiency and growth. However, if politicians or voters have only a short-term decision horizon, it is uncertain whether there are net benefits from the switch to the Euro. The one-off costs of switching to the currency and a transitory increase in unemployment could be short-term effects dominating the short-term gains of the tradables sector where savings in transaction and hedging costs will occur; under a short time horizon the positive effects occurring in the medium run are only partly considered – long term effects are fully ignored.

For society economic welfare U can be assumed to depend on per capita income y, leisure l, public goods g as well as employment and price stability. High rates of unemployment have a negative effect not only on the unemployed but also on the many workers facing uncertainty; i.e. there is fear of a high risk of being laid-off in the future which is the more intense the higher the unemployment rate u is and the higher the share of long-term unemployment (z). Hence the following welfare function could be considered:

$$U = f(y,l,g,u,z,\pi)$$

where the partial derivatives for y, g and l are positive, while those for u, z and π are negative. It will be quite difficult to estimate the welfare gain of Euroland, especially since one might see negative employment effects in the nontradables sector which will have to shrink if governments are forced to reduce government expenditure-GDP ratios because of the Stability and Growth Pact (and because of declining corporate tax revenues). On the positive side one can expect that intra-Euroland inflation differentials will stimulate in high-growth countries – with inflation above Euroland average – liberalization in sheltered industries since this is one of the few policy options to dampen national inflation rates in the new monetary setting of "one size fits all". Such liberalization (eg in Spain, Portugal, Ireland, Netherlands) indeed is likely to reinforce growth via static and dynamic efficiency gains.

3. Price Competition, Real Interest Rates and Investment under EMU

Competition and Pricing

Introducing the Euro in 1999 has raised the transparency of markets and strengthened the integration of markets in the Euro area. This will reinforce competition, which in turn should stimulate firms to invest in process innovations and product innovations on the one hand; on the other hand one may expect a stronger price convergence across Euro countries as a consequence of intensified price arbitrage in the tradables sector. Taking Germany as a benchmark, absolute price levels of tradables are considerably higher in Denmark, Sweden and Finland. The absolute price level is lower in France, Belgium, the Netherlands, Italy, Ireland, the UK, Spain and Portugal (DRESDNER KLEINWORT BENSON, 1998); in the latter three countries tradable prices are only about 4/5 of the German price level. In the pre-Euro single market there certainly is price differentiation across countries where one may expect somewhat smaller prices in low-income countries (Ireland, Spain and Portugal). However, relatively low prices in Belgium, the Netherlands and Italy plus the UK point for Germany to a potential for prices to fall temporarily in the tradables sector while countries with low price levels are likely to face a temporary increase of prices.

In a transition period the real interest rates thus will differ across EU countries where Germany and France are likely to face relatively high rates while the Netherlands, Italy, Ireland, Spain and Portugal will have lower real interest rates (here, we deflate the nominal interest rate by the tradables inflation rate). We assume, of course, that nominal interest rates across Euro countries will be identical. Countries with relatively low real interest rates could benefit in their export sectors from higher investment output ratios, especially when they used to have high real interest ratios in the EMS (I) regime; this is the case of Spain, Ireland, Portugal and Italy. Germany, France, Austria, Belgium and the Netherlands transitorily could face reduced internal investment dynamics, as they are unlikely to experience a significant real interest rate reduction from the introduction of the Euro. In these countries real rates have been low for a rather long time so that currency union will have limited effects on investment of domestic firms. This still leaves open the issue whether or not higher foreign direct investment flows – especially from outside the EU – will raise the investment output ratio in the five core countries. In the 1990s FDI inflows have contributed some 3% to Germany's gross fixed capital formation, while it reached 10% or more in the Netherlands, France, Spain and Portugal. Italy was even worse than Germany, and this is a sign of weakness of Euroland – with the two countries accounting for more than 50% of GDP in Euroland – which faces problems in attracting high FDI inflows in a period of globally rising FDI flows.

One should also wonder about the levels of the overall price index P which is composed not only of tradable goods but of nontradable goods as well (ω=share of nontradables in consumption).

$$P= (P_N)^{\omega} (P_T)^{1-\omega}= P_T (P_N/P_T)^{\omega}$$

From a theoretical point of view it is clear that with falling nominal interest rates there will be a rise of the real EU/Euro money demand M^d/P. This could be compatible with a given money supply growth rate and a once-and-for-all decline in the overall price level, or at a given price level money supply growth can temporarily be higher than in the long run; however, this is so only in combination with a Euro depreciation which could slightly raise the price level of tradables while leaving the equilibrium relative price of tradables to nontradables unchanged. By moving to a higher real per capita money stock the economy will experience a positive welfare and wealth effect. From a portfolio-theoretical perspective this should stimulate demand for real estate and stocks; if higher stock demand mainly falls on the US market, a Euro depreciation will occur. Higher wealth in Euroland should stimulate consumption demand.

Comparing absolute price levels of all goods the findings with respect to high price groups and low price countries are rather similar except that Portugal's price level is almost as high as the German one and the price level of Belgium and

France slightly higher than in Germany. These exceptions point to rather weak competition in the nontradables sector or inefficiencies, which might partly be related to state-owned firms or public monopolies with relatively high prices. Indeed the ratio of people employed in the public sector relative to those in the private sector was lowest with 15% in the Netherlands in 1995 – two points below the US and the UK figure – while Sweden (with 46% up from 26% in 1970), Denmark, Finland, France, Austria, Belgium and Portugal (23%) had much higher figures than Germany, Spain, Italy and Ireland with 18%, 19%, 20% and 23%, respectively (IWD, 1998). While the Netherlands has a strong welfare state including broad public services, government obviously strongly has favored outsourcing which in turn should contribute to stimulating productivity growth and thus to obtaining relatively low price levels in the nontradables sector. With the ongoing deregulation and privatization of network industries, i.e. telecommunications, energy and water in EU countries, there are favorable prospects for improved productivity growth in the nontradables sector. To the extent that nontradables are used as an input in the tradables sector such productivity improvements will also stimulate the expansion of tradables production and thus contribute to higher employment in this sector. The net employment effect could be positive or negative; empirical analysis is needed to shed light on this issue.

Aggregate Investment

By reducing long-term real interest rates in most EU countries monetary union will stimulate private investment and could help to raise public investment as interest payments in the government budget are reduced. As the creation of the ECB and the Euro, respectively, means reducing economic uncertainty, there will be less exchange rate uncertainty for all Euro countries and for some of them reduced variability on the money supply side. This is another reason to expect higher investment output ratios in Euroland. Recent empirical analysis in WELFENS/JUNGMITTAG (1997) suggests that elimination of intra-EU exchange rate variability will raise the investment output ratio in Germany and the Netherlands. Moreover, a significant negative coefficient of money supply variability in Belgium, (West) Germany, Italy, the Netherlands, Denmark, the United Kingdom and Ireland was found which lets one expect that a rather steady monetary policy of the European Central Bank also will stimulate investment; since the money supply will be easier to control in Euroland than in an individual EU country there are good long-term prospects for reduced money supply variability which in turn should translate into a less pronounced business cycle and a higher equilibrium investment-output ratio. As regards prospects for higher investment a counter-effect can be expected from initial uncertainties of market participants with respect to ECB strategies and policy effectiveness. In any case the increase of the investment output ratio can be expected to be rather modest, e.g. for Germany roughly ½ percentage point from the elimination of exchange rate variability. Euroland could record a further increase in the investment output ratio if money supply volatility could be reduced relative to the prior-1999 status. However, many German firms might prefer to rather build new production facilities abroad as price and cost competition has intensified. However, it is unclear whether the ECB will be able to achieve a smooth expansion path for M3 (its target) and M1.

Another aspect related to investment concerns building of houses and the construction industry, respectively. In an integrated and therefore more competitive loan market regulations that used to restrict credit financing of mortgage banks to the national currency area no longer are a barrier to "international financing" within Euroland. For example, the German requirement that liability denomination and asset denomination have to be matched will no longer prevent mortgage banks from Germany to directly enter markets in countries of the Euro zone. At the same time mortgage banks from other Euro countries can be expected to aggressively enter the German market thus leading to easing financing conditions for those who want to build a new house. While housing investment represents 5-8 % of GDP in EU countries one may expect a considerable long-term stimulus for the construction industry except in those EU countries where access to loans traditionally has been rather easy, e.g. in Belgium with low requirements for paid-up capital. Financial market integration will create pressure on EU-wide deregulation, which will largely eliminate the existing segregation of national markets in the long run.

Depreciation Versus Appreciation

One possible scenario for Euroland in the beginning is a nominal and real depreciation vis-à-vis the US dollar and other currencies. An initial Euro depreciation is not unlikely since many Euro skeptics will consider investing in non-Euro currencies, and even for the average optimistic Euro investor, international diversification – being a natural part of optimal portfolio selection – can only be achieved by investing in other currencies in the OECD group where the US dollar and the Swiss franc could become preferred currencies. In the case of such a Euro depreciation one may anticipate not only higher net exports of Euroland but also rising foreign direct investment [FDI] inflows relative to GDP in Euroland; hence higher US, British, Swedish and Swiss FDI to Euro land will contribute to capital formation, technological progress and economic growth in the currency union.

Besides the fact that a Euro depreciation makes US exports to the EU less profitable, the main reason of higher US FDI flows in the context of a dollar appreciation is that in imperfect capital markets equity capital matters. Capital markets are imperfect and not fully efficient (FAMA, 1991) and FROOT/STEIN (1991) have emphasized that capital market imperfections are important for FDI flows. The more equity capital – expressed in terms of the currency of the target country – a potential investor can put up the greater the amount of possible borrowing which can be obtained. A dollar appreciation will translate into higher equity capital – evaluated in Euro terms – of a US firm seeking to acquire a firm in Euroland and hence improved opportunities for successful acquisition in Euroland. A transitory Euro depreciation should therefore stimulate FDI inflows into the Euro area.

4. Transmission Channels of Monetary Policy

As fiscal policy in Euroland is constrained by the Stability and Growth Pact – and the 3% maximum for the budget deficit in normal recessions – it will be important to prudently use policies for structural change and growth on the one hand, i.e. changes in government expenditure priorities over time, and on the other hand monetary policy. The ESCB has set a first money growth target rate of 4.5% in 1999 which assumes a fall in trend velocity of 1% p.a., while the bank wants to avoid inflation and allow sufficient money supply growth to accomodate an output growth rate of 2-2.5%.

The target growth rate for M3 seems to be rather narrow as money supply expansion must not only finance output growth but also the enormous growth of financial market activities. Transactions in financial markets of Euroland are strongly stimulated by monetary union which will above all contribute to more intra-EU mergers & acquisitions and to a Europeanization of the representative private household´s portfolio whose traditional preference for national bonds and stocks will reduce as a consequence of the elimination of the exchange rate risk in Euroland. In larger and more liquid markets there will be more trading, and this absorbs liquidity. As regards M1 money supply growth (in "synthetically aggregated Euroland"; see appendix) in 1997/98 monetary growth accelerated and was close to 9% p.a. in late 1998 which marks an expansionary policy course to the extent that M1 impulses are particularly relevant for the business cycle development. M3 impulses are more relevant for long-term inflation development, and in 1997/98 the M3 growth rate was close to 5% which implies – assuming a two year lag for inflation – an inflation rate close to 1% in 1999. With the ECB adopting in the starting year a growth rate for M3 for 4.5% the ECB has chosen a much too conservative target since it has not taken into account that rising stock market sales will absorb considerable liquidity. The 20% depreciation of the Euro vis-à-vis the dollar in 1999/2000. It is likely to raise inflationary pressure with some time lag.

Monetary policy in Euroland should react rather timely, i.e. in a similar fashion as the US FED during the business cycle if the ECB is to influence output and employment without violating its priority goal of price stability. From this perspective monetary policy transmission mechanisms are important. Monetary policy transmission mechanisms typically work via three different channels: (i) the interest rate mechanism (ii) the credit mechanism and (iii) the exchange rate mechanism; a fourth (iv) is the expectation mechanism which concerns the credibility of the central bank and thus the lag between monetary policy and wage or price adjustments in labor and goods markets. The German Council of Economic Experts (SVR, 1998) has focussed on the first three transmission channels (see also the following table). The investment-GDP ratio differs slightly across EU countries, ranging from 17% to 26% in 1997. From this perspective Austria and Portugal might react more strongly to monetary impulses than other Euroland member countries; as regards the structure of output – with manufacturing industry and construction being rather sensitive with respect to interest rates – a high share of manufacturing value-added in overall production will reinforce the reaction of the economy to changes in the interest rates. Disregarding Luxembourg the highest and lowest shares of manufacturing industry differ by 5.6 points across Euroland member countries. The range for the share of the construction industry is between 4.3% in France and 7.8% in Spain. From this structural perspective Germany, Austria, Portugal and Spain are rather sensitive to interest rate shocks. Another aspect concerns the public debt-GDP ratio where the rather high figures for Belgium and Italy – being reflected also in high interest rate expenditures relative to GDP, namely 7.9 and 9.5%, respectively (twice as high as in other Euroland countries) – are of some special concern. This argument is reinforced by a relatively high share of short-term debt which was rather high in Italy (over 50%) but also was relatively high in France, Spain and Portugal with roughly 30%. One may expect that a period of low interest rates in the Euro starting period will encourage Italy, France, Spain and Portugal to reduce the share of short-term government borrowing so that future exposure to interest rate shocks is smaller than in the past.

The credit mechanism mainly concerns the supply of loans, while the interest rate channel affects the demand side. With rising interest rates the share of risky loans is increasing, and deteriorating credit ratings of many companies in periods of high interest rates further could restrict credit expansion. As regards the potential role of the credit mechanism the share of bank credits in overall enterprise liabilities is crucial. This share is roughly one-third in Euroland countries. Exceptions are Germany and France where the share is 20.7 and 13.0 percent, respectively. Indeed, in France securitization is well advanced. This tendency will be reinforced across Euroland in the medium term as a more integrated and competitive financial market should make securitization more accessible to all firms.

Fig. A2: Growth Rates of M1 and M3

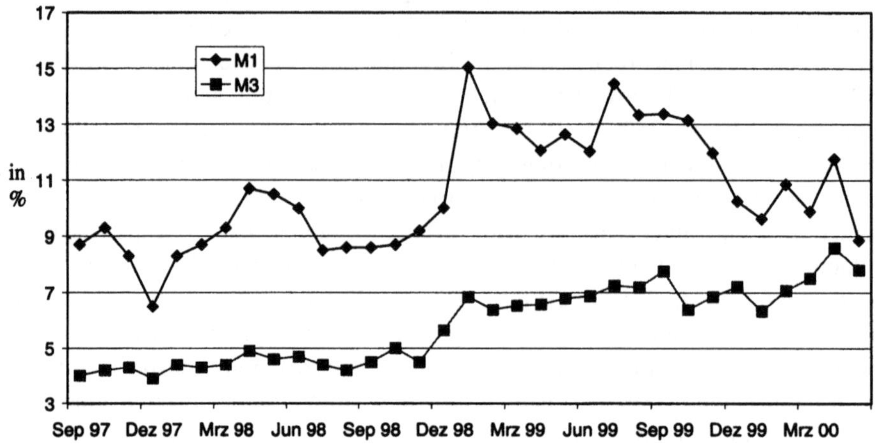

Source: ECB (2000b)

Tab. A1: Selected Real and Financial Indicators for Euroland

	Selected Components of Nominal GDP				Shares of Sectors in GDP	
Country	Private Consumption 1)	Fixed Capital Formation 1)	Government Expenditure 1)	EU-11 Exports 2) 3)	Manufacturing	Const-ruction
	% of Nominal GDP					
	1997			1996		
Belgium	62.5	17.6	14.5	25.3 a)	18.2	4.8
Germany	64.9	20.1	12.0	14.1	23.4	5.9
Finland	53.0	16.9	20.7	24.0	22.4	5.1
France	60.3	17.1	19.4	11.1	18.9	4.3
Ireland	52.1	18.7	14.1	40.2	n.a.	4.5 b)
Italy	61.5	16.8	16.3	11.5	20.2	5.0
Luxembourg	53.1	22.4	13.3	n.a.	15.4 b)	7.0 b)
Netherlands	60.1	20.5	14.1	19.4	17.8	5.0 b)
Austria	55.7	24.2	19.4	12.5	19.8	7.4
Portugal	64.0	25.6	18.6	8.0	22.5 b)	6.2 b)
Spain	62.4	20.3	15.9	7.9	17.8	7.8

Tab. A1: Selected Real and Financial Indicators for Euroland (cont.)

Country	Indicators for Public Debt				Indicators for Enterprise Financing	
	Debt	Interest Payments	Debt vis-a-vis Residents	Short-term Debt	Total Bank Loans	Short-term Bank Loans
	In % of Nominal GDP		In % of Total Debt		In Relation to Total Enterprise Liabilities	
	1997				1995	
Belgium	122.2	7.9	78.2 c)	24.6	28.8	10.5
Germany	61.3	3.7	71.1 c)	18.5 c)	20.7 d)	12.7 d)
Finland	55.8	5.4	36.8	19.1	31.6 e)	10.6 e)
France	58.0	3.6	86.7	29.4	13.0	6.3
Ireland	66.3	4.3	64.1	8.9	n.a.	n.a.
Italy	121.6	9.5	79.0	49.4	33.8	20.5
Luxembourg	6.7	0.3	85.1	0.1	n.a.	n.a.
Netherlands	72.1	5.3	82.3 c)	6.7	25.1	11.5
Austria	66.1	4.1	71.3	10.7	n.a. f)	19.3
Portugal	62.0	4.3	75.3 c)	33.1	33.8 g)	13.5 g)
Spain	68.8	4.5	78.5	30.6	34.0	12.4

1) European System of National Accounts (ESVG 79).
2) Extratrade: Without trade with the EMU countries.
3) Constructed from the database of the harmonized enterprise accounts of the European Commission (BACH - Bank for the Accounts of Companies Harmonized).
a) Inclusive of Luxembourg.
b) 1995.
c) 1996.
d) Only manufacturing (exclusive of energy and water supply) and trade. Data exclusive of the GDR.
e) Only manufacturing (exclusive of construction)
f) BACH does not include data of long-term liabilities.
g) Only manufacturing, traffic and communication.
Source: SVR (1998), Jahresgutachten 1998/99, p. 168

The exchange rate mechanism of monetary policy is related to the fact that a rise of interest rates will cause a nominal and real depreciation which is of particular significance for countries with a high share of exports and imports in

GDP. More strictly, the exchange rate impact will become less significant for those rather open economies in Euroland with a high share of intra-Euroland trade. However, for countries with a high share of extra-EU exports the exchange rate mechanism will remain important; in this respect, it is crucial for the Netherlands (19.4% share of extra-EU exports in overall exports), Finland (24%), Belgium (25.3%) and Ireland (40.2%); less important is this channel for France, Italy, Spain and Portugal. Germany (with a share of 14.1%) is in the middle of the extremes.

As regards empirical evidence Portugal and Spain reacted relatively little to interest rate shocks in the past which might be less attributable to structural aspects of the two economies than to reflection of the fact that in countries with a historically high interest rate volatility an interest rate change of one percentage point has a smaller impact than the same interest rate change in countries with low interest rate variability. In Euroland the interest rate volatility will converge strongly across countries so that Spain and Portugal are likely to respond similarly to other EU countries in the future.

In addition to these reflections of the German Council of Economic Experts one may add two important observations. (i) The real exchange rate effect for Euroland countries with a high share of inward and outward FDI in overall investment is crucial. A real depreciation of the Euro will stimulate foreign direct investment inflows relative to GDP (more US investment flows into Euroland) – according to the FROOT-STEIN argument – and it will reduce FDI outflows as acquiring firms e.g. in the US become more expensive for Euroland firms. (ii) A rise of interest rates in Euroland will affect investment of firms less than a similar monetary restriction in the past as small and medium sized firms will increasingly benefit from a more competitive financial market in Euroland. Hence even relatively young and small firms will be able to issue bonds in the Euro capital market. The impact on the quality of all outstanding bonds in Euroland will be a slight deterioration of the average bond rating – indeed Euroland will witness the emergence of a US-type "junk bonds market". Disregarding this effect the interest rate margin for banks will reduce in the more competitive financial markets of Euroland.

Given the sluggish business development in 1999 – the starting year of the Euro – and the reduced interest rate sensitivity of the economy of Euroland one should hope that the ECB will reduce short-term interest rates in several steps in 1999/2000. To do so will be rather difficult for the ECB if there is much political noise about interest rate reductions; indeed the ECB in such a case is likely to be quite hesitant with regard to an interest rate reduction in order to demonstrate its political independence. A prudent policy of interest rate reduction in 1999/2000 need not entail a strong devaluation of the Euro to the extent that such a monetary policy is combined with prudent growth policies – an adequate change of fiscal policies – and employment-enhancing wage policies. To achieve consensus on such a policy assignment might, however, be quite difficult in Euroland.

5. EMU, Capital Markets and Growth of New Firms

Survey results from and actual behavior of industrial firms in the run-up to the single market project indicate that intensified price competition leads to international relocation of production and intensified innovation. Low wage EU countries have benefited particularly from the single market project as is obvious from very high per capita inflows of Spain and Portugal after 1987. With the Euro pricing competition further intensifying in the single market, however, and with systemic transformation in eastern Europe and expected accession of some transforming countries ante portas, one may anticipate that EU firms from high wage countries will be eager to not only consider intra-EU relocations of standardized production but also a wider relocation which could include eastern Europe. In this case Germany, Austria, Italy and Finland would be the major beneficiaries because rising potential output and increasing real GNP in eastern Europe will particularly stimulate the exports of EU countries with a strong east European export orientation. The logic of the gravity equation can be applied here.

Facing the Euro, multinational firms in Euroland will pursue strategies of international M&As in the Community while rationalizing production which implies some labor shake out. New jobs might be created in the service sector in EU countries, but one should keep in mind that this will go along with a slow but systemic fall in the aggregate investment-output ratio since services are less capital intensive than manufacturing industry. With large industrial establishments being closed in many EU member countries there is a need for counterbalancing growth of the nontradables sector (service sector plus construction industry) plus creation of new firms in both this sector and the tradables sector. We therefore will focus on capital market perspectives associated with the introduction of the Euro and the ECB, respectively, but also raise the issue of venture capitalism in Western Europe.

With a fully integrated single EU market and increased price transparency firms have on the one hand an incentive to fully exploit community-wide opportunities for economies of scale. On the other hand, firms have incentives to replace price differentiation in accordance with national markets – traditionally separated from each other via exchange rate risk – via strategies which segregate markets according to product varieties and corresponding customer profiles. Product differentiation will go along with product innovation so that higher R&D expenditures relative to value-added can be expected. As firms aim to raise their R&D intensity the financing of innovations becomes more important.

Financing innovations via lending raises specific problems because of the information asymmetry between banks and the innovating firms which, of course, have a superior knowledge about the technological merits and the commercial risks of product and process innovations. In continental EU countries it would be desirable to raise the equity capital-debt ratio of firms in order to facilitate the financing of innovations. If firms can put up more equity capital they will find it easier to finance innovations, and certainly both the end of the Cold War and the general long term trend towards globalization (WELFENS/ADDISON/AUDRETSCH/GRUPP, 1998) make a stronger EU specialization in high technology seem to be reasonable. Once the respective firms have established a reputation as a successful innovator they should face no major problems in financing innovations via the stock market (WELFENS/WOLF, 1997).

Venture Capitalism and Capital Structure

Venture capital is crucial for Germany and continental EU countries which traditionally have relied on a bank-dominated financing of investment and innovation. In 1996 DM 6.6 bill. of venture capital was available in Germany which is roughly 1/8 of the US equivalent of roughly DM 50 bill. p.a.; German figures thus were slightly less than one-half of US per capita figures; the UK recorded an impressive DM 22 bill. while venture capital in France reached DM 9.4 bill. In 1998/99 the situation in Germany had improved considerably since overall venture capital funds had strongly increased – not least for seed financing; however, relative to the US where one has also witnessed a venture capital boom there is still a considerable gap.

While seed financing and start-up financing dominate the US venture capital business – i.e. young innovative firms attract most of the venture capital – the situation in Germany is characterized by 60% of funds going into already existing firms eager to finance further expansion; according to BVK only 3% of venture capital is available already before the creation of a new firm (seed financing) and 7% at the start of new companies (start-up financing). While US venture capitalism has a high share of 61% geared towards high technology, the share in Germany is only 7%. In 1996/97 there was considerable growth of German venture capital funds which supported the growth of new biotechnology firms. Such firms could also benefit from the New Market at the German stock exchange which has entered a cooperation with similar new stock markets for dynamic newcomers.

Raising the equity capital/debt ratio of firms in continental EU countries is also useful in order to make firms more weatherproof against the business cycles. It is well-known that a main reason for business failures in continental EU countries is the relatively low equity capital/debt ratio. The gradual build-up of high unemployment in Western Europe indeed partly reflects a capital structure problem of firms; with each successive recession new firms as well as established firms go bankrupt. Given the low birth rate of firms in the EU, the relatively high death rate of firms is worrisome. While the death rate of US firms is higher than that in the EU its net birth rate certainly testifies to higher US entrepreneurial dynamics. Switzerland, the US and the UK show much better figures in terms of the capital structure. Euro firms also need higher equity capital-debt ratios because a strict ECB monetary regime rules out that high inflation policies could save firms which face liquidity problems.

While US and EU figures of overall investment in venture capital were roughly equal – each reaching about $ 5.5 bill. in 1995 – the US enjoys a clear advantage in venture capital financing of new firms. The average size of seed capital was more than three times the EU figures, and the number of seed and start-up investment projects represented 26% in the US but only 5.7% in the EU in 1995 (EUROPEAN COMMISSION, 1997b, p.118). For Western Europe (EU-15 except Luxembourg plus Iceland, Norway and Switzerland) the distribution of stages in percent of venture capital investment was as follows in 1995: Seed financing 2.5%; start-up 16.5%; replacement 6.8%; buy-out 21.5%; expansion 52.8%. The share of start-up and seed financing reached 13.3% in Germany, while expansion and buy-out accounted for 66.5% and 20.2%, respectively. Compared to Germany the Netherlands and Italy had a slightly higher share for start-up and seed financing, namely 16.3% and 17.7%, respectively. The UK had a very low share of 1% for start-up and seed financing while buy-out financing dominated with a share of 70.3%. France also had a low share of start-up and seed financing, namely 3.26%, while expansion, replacement and buy-out financing recorded shares of 35.9%, 21.2% and 39.7%, respectively. In Spain expansion financing dominated in 1995. As regards the sectoral breakdown information technology dominated with a share of 46% in the US (EU 16%) while non-technology venture capital investment dominated in the EU with 76% (EU 16%). This also contributed to the EU's negative trade balance of $ 35 bill. in high technology goods compared to a combined US-Japanese surplus of $ 150 bill. in 1996.

It therefore is obvious that relatively low EU capital productivity as well as West European unemployment problems are partly due to lack of venture capital financing and to a lack of technology-oriented seed and start-up financing. As regards Germany the link to the labor market is fairly obvious since high technology start-ups have about 12 employees while non-technology firms employ about half as many. At the same time it cannot be overlooked that about half of EU unemployed lack formal training and higher education so that skill upgrading and expansion of the service sector will have to be pursued in addition to improved high-technology and long term R&D policies (WELFENS, 1998a; WELFENS/AUDRETSCH/ ADDISON/GRUPP, 1998)

6. Relative Prices, Factor Rewards and Real Convergence

Factor Prices and EMU

The introduction of the Euro will reduce the relative price of tradables since it is the tradables sector where the switch to a single currency brings high savings of costs. In the nontradables sector there are no immediate impulses for price reductions. We assume that the tradables are produced mainly by skilled workers and capital so that this sector is relatively skill intensive and capital intensive; the nontradables sector (construction, personal and government services) is using unskilled labor more intensively. In the spirit of the Stolper-Samuelson theorem – which, however, refers to two tradables (with a rise of the relative goods price the price of that factor which is used relatively intensively in the production of this good will increase) – we can state the paradox hypothesis that unskilled labor will particularly benefit from EMU.

It is true that unskilled labor in Europe has been a loser in the process of economic globalization starting in the 1980s, but this is mainly because the economic opening-up of China and the expansion of some Asian and Latin American newly industrializing countries has stimulated trade in standardized production which uses unskilled labor intensively. According to the Ryczynski theorem – based on given output prices – the output of the good intensively using the more abundant factor will decline. This suggests that output of tradables using skilled workers and capital equipment intensively will increase. As output in the product cycle always will first increase in technologically leading economies – above all the US – the main winner of the globalization process should be the US (and some other main source countries of foreign direct investment).

Real Convergence, Foreign Direct Investment and Innovation Policies

A final remark with respect to distribution effects concerns the issue of foreign direct investment in a spatial ownership perspective. If ownership of capital is not distributed equally in the world economy – and it certainly is not – the Heckscher-Ohlin-Samuelson theorem (suggesting international equalization of factor rewards and thus real income convergence) is rather uninteresting for at least two reasons: first, in a world of MNCs which base their market leadership on product and process innovations, production functions at home and abroad will differ, and this is inconsistent with the HOS approach; secondly, in a two-country-world in which – for ease of exposition – country I fully owns the capital stock in country II, even the case of identical production functions (with identical population figures at home and abroad) will not lead to convergent GNPs per capita. With a production function Y=Kexp(ß)Lexp(1-ß) and similarly Y*=K*exp(ß*)L*exp(1-ß*) we would have identical gross domestic products at home, i.e. country I, and abroad in country II. But GNP in the source country of foreign investment, namely country I, is GDP plus ßY*, while GNP abroad is Y*-ßY*. The assumption of identical GDPs at home and abroad then leads for the case of ß=1/3 to a divergence in per capita GNPs of 2:1 in favor of the source country (WELFENS, 1994). While the Heckscher-Ohlin theorem implies an international equalization of factor rewards, in the nonneoclassical world of multinational companies – or foreign direct investment – there will be no per capita convergence. In our perspective by implication it is clear that international per capita differences are mainly related to divergent abilities of countries to become major source countries of foreign direct investment.

Taking into account the DUNNING approach to foreign direct investment which has emphasized owner-specific advantages – mainly technological leadership but also leadership in soft skills related to organization or marketing – as the basis for successful multinationalization, one must emphasize that real international income convergence is strongly related to poor countries developing technological leadership in at least some niches and the nurturing of indigenous entrepreneurs willing to undertake investment abroad. From this perspective the Community´s innovation policy as well as the national R&D policy in EU member states becomes quite important as are programs designed to stimulate entrepreneurship. As regards Community R&D programs a recurrent shortcoming is that such programs are relatively small – at least in comparison to EU agricultural subsidies – and that there is hardly any emphasis on the user of innovations; there is too much orientation towards basic R&D and insufficient interest in the demand side. This is in stark contrast to the US approach to R&D promotion.

7. Labor Markets, Mobility and Unemployment

In western Europe labor mobility is lower than in the US, and it has declined over time. This is a phenomenon which is not well understood despite a broad discussion in the literature (GROS/HEFEKER, 1998; GOTTSCHALK, 1997; CORNEO, 1995; EICHENGREEN, 1994; DANTHINE/HUNT, 1994; DEERESSIN/FATAS, 1995; CALMFORS, 1997; GRÜNER/HEFEKER, 1998). While one might argue that rising female labor participation rates compound the problem of labor mobility in the case of a negative economic shock to a region, the US experience in the 1980s and 1990s is a counter-example: participation ratios increased strongly while full employment was achieved and maintained. At the same time this observation would not be surprising if regional and sectoral shocks had reduced in comparison to the 1960s and 1970s or if a given intensity of shocks went along with increased wage flexibility. A negative shock to a region will not result in lay-offs if there is sufficient wage flexibility or if each region is so diversified that mobility within a given region allows maintaining full employment. Finally, one has to take into account the simple fact that jobs typically are lost in capital-intensive industry while new jobs are created in skill-intensive services or in services with low capital intensity. If new firms mainly were created in depressed industrial areas – start-up firms could be attracted by declining and low wages as well as tax concessions and public grants – one also would have a mechanism that allows reconciling regional shocks to industry with sustained full employment. However, it is rather unlikely that depressed regions are naturally the favored breeding ground of newly created firms. Instead most newly established firms are likely to prefer dynamic regions with high per capita growth and a large pool of skilled workers.

Impediments to regional labor mobility are caused in several EU countries by tax labor laws: e.g. in Germany there is a 3.5 % property acquisition tax, and in Belgium a similar tax to be paid when buying a house is progressively related to the asset value and can reach up to 20 %. Such taxes slow down regional mobility.

As regards motivation to move it is clear that regional policies of the type applied both within most EU countries and via supranational structural funds discourage labor mobility. Income differentials across regions are therefore lower than productivity differentials. Governments in Germany, Belgium, Italy and other EU countries have used regional redistribution schemes to attenuate interregional income differentials, and thereby they have indirectly reduced labor mobility. Given the abolition of the exchange rate instrument within the Euro area there is, of course, need to raise labor mobility. This supports the case for a reduction of national and supranational EU policies. Higher wage flexibility also is desirable in a monetary union. Indeed a new policy option could be to reinforce built-in stabilization of the economic system, e.g. by employee ownership which would pay out dividends to workers mainly in recessions. Governments could encourage such ownership plans by adequate tax laws.

While from the individual's perspective the marginal costs of moving from one region – normally the problem is from a high unemployment region with depressed asset prices to a low unemployment region with high asset prices – to another is high, the marginal benefits often are rather low. Private costs of moving away consist of giving up a familiar local network of friends which amounts to a depreciation of the stock of the individual's "social capital" which can be assumed to enter the utility function with a positive sign. Indeed, countries with a rather high labor mobility tend to have a higher divorce ratio than low mobility countries, and the stress of divorce certainly then is part of the mobility costs. Costs also occur in the form of higher rents which might have to be paid in the new location. Finding a new job and hence enjoying higher disposable income is the main aspect on the benefit side while for society there are additional external benefits, namely in terms of reduced unemployment compensation and a reduced crime rate, i.e. less uncertainty of consumption which is welfare enhancing. Moreover, each unemployed worker finding a job reduces fear of unemployment of those who have a job. In Germany the budgetary costs of unemployment without negative external costs were some DM 142 bill. in 1995 when there were some 5 million unemployed. In addition to the cost of ECU 14000 per unemployed there are external costs of immobility in the form of higher expenditures for crime protection and higher health care costs. Taking into account private costs and benefits of moving away from point O would establish radius R_0 while the social optimum is given by point B and R_1, respectively (see Figure 1). It would thus be adequate to subsidize labor mobility (by BC) if this could contribute to lower unemployment. Co-financing of such schemes by the EU might be useful. The traditional EU tax agenda (GENSER et al., 1998) should thus be enlarged. The justification for an EU Commission initiative in favor of subsidization of labor mobility stems from the supranational opportunity cost of non-mobility at the national level, i.e. higher EU structural transfers.

Fig. A3: Marginal Labor Mobility Costs and Private (u') and Social (u'S) Benefits

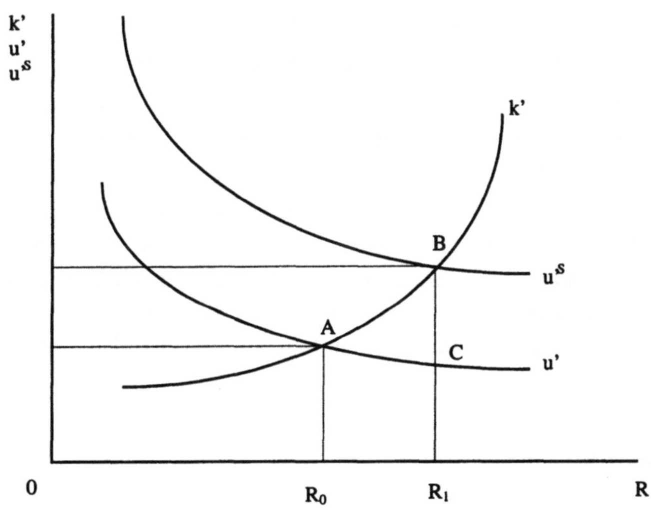

8. Implications for Economic Policies and Budget Consolidation

Reducing expenditures on regional policies will help to reduce the deficit-GDP ratios on the one hand, and on the other hand, new subsidies for encouraging labor mobility will be an offsetting effect; the same holds if property acquisition taxes were abolished which would be useful to achieve higher mobility. To the extent that higher investment-GDP ratios and increasing employment can be achieved the budget consolidation process is influenced favorably. One should emphasize that – given the requirements of the stability and growth pact – it will be crucial to reduce deficits to figures around zero in periods of economic upswings; otherwise there is insufficient room for fiscal policy to combat recessions. Higher government expenditures on public investment and education plus more innovation support are required for growth and employment.

EMU could be the start of a virtuous circle in Europe in which overdue reforms of the labor markets and capital markets support economic growth, higher productivity and employment as well as catching-up vis-à-vis the US. Labor mobility and wage flexibility are politically sensitive issues, but one may expect that trade unions and workers will be prepared to accept a new deal if there are reasonable prospects of reducing unemployment and new initiatives for employee ownership programs. Problems could, however, come from a bias in technological progress which – based on US and EU evidence – seems to favor skilled labor. Unskilled workers will suffer from relatively declining wages. EU governments – eager to reduce debt-GDP ratios – could be reluctant to raise expenditures on education, training and retraining which indeed is required to improve employability in Euroland; and to limit the political problems of biased technological progress leading to a rise of the skilled-unskilled wage ratio.

The consolidation effects in the 1990s were reinforced by falling interest rates in many Euro candidate countries. However, there is always a risk of adverse international or domestic interest rate shocks.

Macroeconomic policy analysis at present is rather conventional and should be widened to include structural indicators for both labor markets and capital markets as well as newcomer and FDI dynamics. Western Europe has a long way to go to overcome both the unemployment overhang from the 1970s and 1980s and to successfully cope with the challenges of economic globalization (WELFENS et al., 1998).

9. Looming EU Protectionism?

Within Euroland some countries – notably France and Italy – seem to favor a Euro depreciation strategy as a means to solve domestic unemployment problems. With the creation of Euroland the EU will increasingly perceive itself as a specific identity and therefore could indeed consider options to exploit its leverage as a large economy in the world market. Following the standard literature on optimum tariffs it is obvious that a large country could improve its terms of trade via imposing an import tariff, the optimum being the inverse of the import supply elasticity E according to traditional trade theory. However, the traditional optimum tariff theory does not consider the role of foreign direct investment. Taking into account the role of outward foreign direct investment (WELFENS, 1998b) one finds for large countries which are major source countries of foreign direct investment that the optimum tariff rate is smaller than suggested by traditional approaches. The optimum import tariff is (1/E)(1-h)x*, where x* stands for the export-GDP ratio of the exporting country (country II) and h is the share of capital owned by multinational companies (from importing country I) in the exporting country's export sector. The basic reason behind the modified optimum tariff rule is that import tariffs imposed by a country which is a major source country of foreign direct investment tend to reduce the profits accruing to subsidiaries abroad whose production partly goes to the markets in the country where the parent company is located. Since Euroland is a major source country of FDI and a considerable share of its imports actually is from subsidiaries abroad which are owned by EU firms, one may anticipate limited tariff protectionism on the part of Euroland.

The protectionist issues could become more important, however, in a transatlantic economic setting if conflicts in the field of exchange rate policy or of monetary policy coordination should emerge in a way which leads either the US or the EU to resort to import restrictions as a bargaining chip in order to achieve concessions in other policy areas.

Having lost many protectionist options due to the WTO rules and EU monitoring of subsidies, the option of a Euro depreciation – including talking down the Euro or weakening it by uncooperative behavior of some ministers of finance – could be politically attractive if Euroland were unable to restore full employment.

10. Real Exchange Rate Aspects

Short-term exchange rate dynamics are strongly affected by international interest rate differentials, exchange rate expectations and stock market developments, and in the long run other aspects are more crucial: the (transatlantic) inflation differential, growth rate differentials and prospects for the current account balance. Euroland's current account position was slightly positive in 1999 – showing a deterioration compared to the preceding years. The US current account position has been negative for the whole second half of the 1990s and the US current account deficit shows a long-term increase, with the absolute figure close to $ 400 bill. in 1999 and even $ 500 bill. in 2000 and 2001 which would exceed 5% of US GDP. The real devaluation of the Euro and the Yen in 1999 has contributed to prospects of a rising US current account deficit in the future, and, more important, the largest bilateral deficits – vis-a-vis China, Mexico and Japan – are likely to further increase: China's export sector is expanding, Mexico's modernization of the supply-side (partly with US foreign direct investment inflows) and Japan's sluggish domestic demand all contribute to rising US imports. From a fundamental perspective there is a favorable potential for US growth since the US patenting record has improved relative to its main competitors and since the US economy enjoys other elements for high long term growth – growth rates above 2 percent over a long time period can be dubbed high in leading OECD countries.

While the depreciation of the Euro in 1999/2000 raises some concerns in Euroland since continuous depreciation could bring about a risk premium for the euro and reinforces resistance of the UK – with its important financial centre London – to join Euroland. The political acceptance of euro coins and euro notes also could be weakened.

However, the depreciation of the Euro is likely to be transitory to the extent that monetary union in Western Europe naturally stimulates international/global diversification in the sense that merging two EU currencies, say DM and Lira, will encourage more investment of Euroland investors outside the monetary union: This is so because a currency union which „merges" DM and Lira will bring about a harmonization of the Italian and German business cycles and a uniform interest rate for Germany-Italy so that portfolio investment of German investors in Italy will be reduced (and that of Italian investors in Germany who also stand to reap less gains from diversification than before); from the perspective of a Euroland investor utility gains from international diversification can no longer be achieved through cross-border investment in Euroland, rather the share of investment in non-Euroland countries – eg Switzerland, UK and the US – will have to be raised in a portfolio optimization approach which aims at balancing risks and returns. More formally, if the optimum long term international portfolio O*** prior to the start of the Euro would be given by a combination of investment in liquid assets M of countries I, II, III and IV – that is $O^{***} = M_I \exp \beta_1 M_{II} \exp \beta_2 M_{III} \exp \beta_3 M_{IV} \exp \beta_4$ – the optimum portfolio after creating a monetary union (dubbed union country V) between country I and II will be characterized by a higher share of investment in M_{III} and M_{IV} (new optimum portfolio $O^{***\prime} = M_V \exp \beta_o M_{III} \exp \beta_{3'} M_{IV} \exp \beta_{4'}$ where $\beta_o < \beta_1 + \beta_2$). This implies a structural transitory depreciation of the euro until a new global portfolio equilibrium has been achieved. An offsetting effect comes from a potential gradual increase in Euroland´s growth rate (eg monetary union reduces transaction costs and raises regional trade and output growth) and the rate of return of Euroland assets, respectively – in particular stocks – so that investors from outside euroland would have a stronger incentive to hold assets of countries I+II. The international net reallocation effect in favor of the dollar creates capital gains in the US which will translate into a rise of the relative price of nontradables in the US which in turn should stimulate transatlantic foreign direct investment in the US nontradables sector. The relative rise of US nontradables prices will cause output in the US tradables sector to reduce so that the US current account deficit will increase; this is indeed what is observed in 1999/2000.

In mid-2000 it seems that the dollar is set to reach record highs against almost all currencies so that the depreciation of the euro is not indicating a fundamental weakness of European Monetary Union. Moreover, the DM – which had stages of depreciations and appreciations (see appendix) hardly would have shown any different behavior in 1999/2000 had EMU not existed – under a hypthetical monetary exchange rate system I a serious crisis would have been likely in 2000 since the oil price shock is asymmetric for EU countries (on EMS dynamics see BOHN, 2000). Based on purchasing power parity the euro dollar exchange rate should be about 0.95 dollar per euro so that a rate close to 0.8 would be a strong deviation from a long term equilibrium exchange rate. Only coordinated intervention of the ECB, the Fed and the Japanese Central Bank would make sense. However, one cannot rule out that the structural lead of the US in computer density and the use of the internet implies a medium term US lead in economic growth which is equivalent to a structural appreciation of the dollar in the context of net US capital inflows. Net FDI inflows increased in 1998-2000.

As regards oil price dynamics OECD countries´ governments have failed to promote the use of future markets. Chip cards could make it possible for truckers of company X to buy gas at the pump at individual future prices. Tax incentives could encourage trucking companies to buy most gas in future markets so that price developments would be smoothened over time. EU politicians should take action. Smoothening of oil prices via increased use of future markets is highly desirable since this also would contribute to more stability and higher growth worldwide.

11. Summary and Conclusions

EMU offers considerable potential benefits for EU countries. The Euro will start at a period of low inflation rates and low structural public deficits, but there are high unemployment rates in most Euro countries. "Restoring full employment" deserves serious efforts on the side of economic policymakers as well as trade unions and employers´ organizations.

From a normative perspective it is clearly desirable to reinforce the role of equity capital and of stock markets, respectively, in order to foster innovation, growth and employment on the one hand, and on the other hand to strengthen firms' ability to better weather the storm of recessions and thus to reduce the number of jobs lost during an economic downswing.

There are several long-term issues of the Euro not covered here. Among the most important problems is the future eastern EU enlargement and the approach of accession states. One can find arguments in favor of flexible exchange rates in postsocialist transforming economies, especially the fact that currency competition and competition among monetary regimes is a disciplinary force urgently needed in eastern Europe's economies with their free-wheeling interest groups (e.g. HEFEKER, 1995).

Appendix A

The True Welfare Costs of Inflation

In Euroland – here for simplicity Italy with a high nominal interest rate i* plus Germany with a traditionally low interest rate of i, i.e. country II and I in the following Fig. – the nominal interest rate probably will be lower after 1999 than previously compared to the average interest rate of the two countries. The interest rate in country II will fall to the level of i1 once monetary union is introduced; for simplicity we assume that monetary union will have a zero inflation rate so that nominal and real interest rates will be identical. The downward interest rate convergence at the start of monetary union is the interest rate reduction effect. Anticipation of EMU could even lead to a fall of the interest rate in the run-up to EMU.

Fig. A2: Demand for Money, Euro Interest Rate Convergence and Welfare Effects

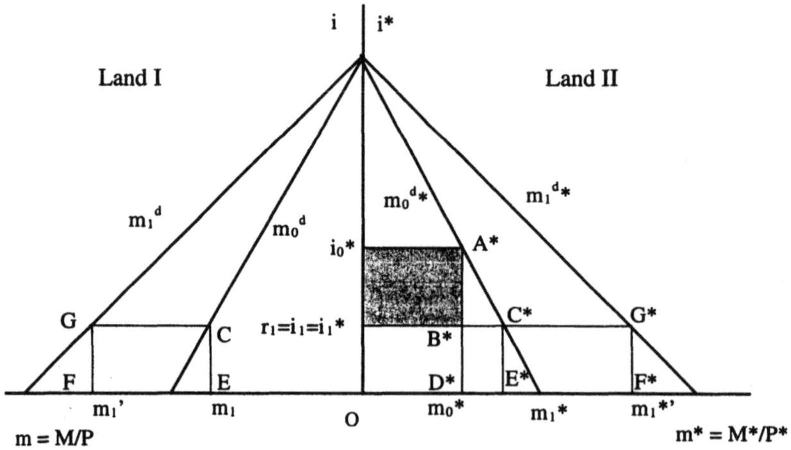

The real welfare loss H* from inflation (correspondingly the gain from price stability) is in a static perspective:

$H^* = r^*\ dm^* + 0.5\ \pi^*\ dm^*$ or $H^*/Y^* = (r^* + 0.5\ \pi^*)\ \varepsilon^*_{m,i}\ [m^*/Y^*]$. (1)

We assume a real interest rate $r^* = 0.04$, an inflation rate $\pi^* = 0.1$, an absolute interest elasticity (equal to the inflation rate elasticity) of $\varepsilon^*_{m,i} = 0.05$ and

$m^*/Y^* = 0.5$; then H^*/Y^* is roughly 1/4 % of GDP. If the inflation risk should increase under EMU in country I (or II) the real demand for money would reduce (see ROTHER, 1997). By implication the credibility of the ECB is crucial if the regime switch is to have a positive welfare effect. In principle the switch to monetary union can go along with a rise or a fall of the interest elasticity.

Taking into account the interest rate reduction effect of EMU, the real money demand M^d/P (for short $M/P=m$) in the currency union will be higher than previously. Money demand should mainly increase in the country which previously had a high inflation rate. The rise in the real demand for money will lead to a temporary excess demand in the money market which can be eliminated by increasing exports of goods or the sale of bonds and equities to foreigners within the EU (assuming an anticipation effect to work, this still takes place within the EMS-I-regime).

The real money demand in Germany might also increase, namely if the interest elasticity of Germany is rising. The demand for money will increase as the demand schedule rotates outwards; at the convergence interest rate we have m_1' instead of m_1 in country I and $m_1^{*\prime}$ instead of m_1^* in country II). The rise of real money balances from m_0^* to m_1^* abroad, i.e. in country II, is associated with a positive welfare effect. The gain corresponds to the triangle A*B*C* plus the rectangular surface B*C*E*D*. Government will forego the inflation tax revenue equivalent to the shaded area. In the traditional textbook perspective this shaded area is considered to be a mere redistribution effect in the sense that a positive inflation rate imposes in a non-growing economy a tax burden of πm which implies that the private sector is giving up resources at the equivalent of πm but will obtain a correspondingly higher supply of public goods (or would enjoy offsetting income tax reductions). This pure redistribution effect, however, means overlooking the divergences in productivity; if one realistically assumes that productivity in the government sector is smaller than in the private sector the inflation tax is not neutral and equation (1) amounts to an understatement of the true welfare costs of inflation. Let us assume that the divergence in factor productivity is 1/5; then the additional gain from a move to price stability is equivalent $0.2\pi^* m^*/Y^*$ (with the parameters chosen, this is 1% of GDP). If the productivity differential were 50%, then half of the shaded area A*B*i*1i*o would be a net welfare gain from moving towards price stability.

If the interest elasticity is increasing with the move towards the Euro and price stability, respectively, in country II we will also have an additional gain of the surface C*G*F*E*. In the noninflationary country I only the positive welfare effect of CEFG is observed. If one assumes that the income elasticity were unity one could use in the diagram m/Y instead of Y.

If one considers money primarily as a consumption good (in a broader sense) which saves time for households and brings a gain in prestige and security for the individual, private households are main winners of the switch to the Euro. If, however, money is mainly considered to be an input factor and a production factor, respectively, switching to the Euro will raise the productivity of complementary production factors and thereby lead to a higher production potential. With a given price level and sticky prices, respectively, the ECB could temporarily raise the money supply growth rate without causing inflation; the additional money supply would be absorbed by the economy where economic agents want to raise the stock of real money balances.

Fig. A3: Business Failures

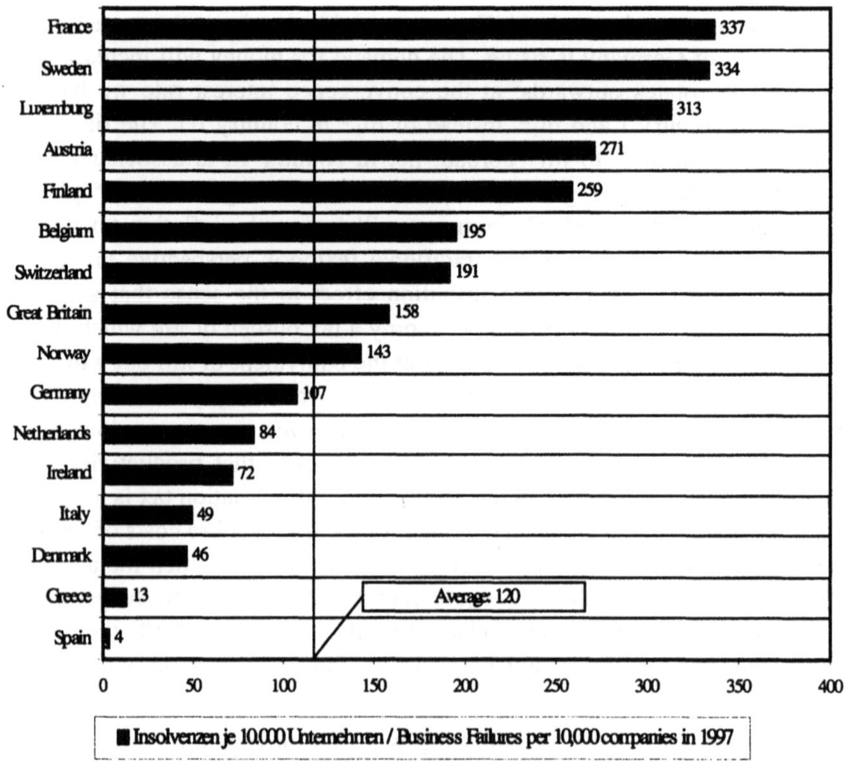

Source: Institut der deutschen Wirtschaft/Creditreform

Tab. A2: Performance of Member States in Relation to Convergence

Current performance of the Member States in relation to convergence*								
	Inflation	Interest rates	General government budgetary position					Exchange rate
	Harmonised indices of consumer prices	Long-term interest rates (2)	Debt/GDP ratio		Deficit/GDP ratio		Debt/GDP ratio	Participation in the ERM (Feb. 1998)
	Jan.97-Dec.97[1]	Jan.97-Dec.97[3]	1996	1997[5]	1996	1997	⊗97/93	
B	1.5	5.8	130.0	122.2 (-)	3.4	(2.1)	12.9	yes
DK	2.0	6.3	70.2	64.1(-)	1.6	0.7	17.9	yes
D	1.5	5.6	60.7	61.3 (+)	3.8	2.7	13.3	yes
EL	5.4	9.9[4]	111.8	108.7 (-)	7.5	4.0	-2.9	no
E	1.9	6.4	69.6	68.3 (-)	4.4	2.6	8.3	yes
F	1.3	5.6	56.2	58.0 (+)	4.1	3.0	12.7	yes
IRL	1.2	6.3	72.8	66.3 (-)	-0.9	-0.9	-29.5	yes
I	1.9	6.9	123.7	121.6 (-)	6.7	2.7	3.5	yes
L	1.4	5.6	6.4	6.7 (+)	-1.8	-1.7	0.6	yes
NL	1.9	5.6	78.5	72.1 (-)	2.4	1.4	-8.5	yes
A	1.2	5.7	70.0	66.1 (-)	3.9	2.5	3.4	yes
P	1.9	6.4	65.6	62.0 (-)	4.1	2.5	-1.1	yes
FIN	1.2	6.0	58.7	55.8 (-)	2.6	0.9	-2.2	yes
S	1.8	6.6	58,7	75.6 (+)	3.6	1.6	-0.2	no
UK	1.9	7.1	54.5	53.4 (-)	4.4	2.6	4.8	no
EUR 15	1.7	6.2						

* Based on the tentative operational definitions of the Maastricht Treaty convergence criteria as presented in the Commission's 1996 convergence report.

[1] Inflation: arithmetic average of twelve monthly harmonised Indices of Consumer Prices (HICP) relative to the arithmetic average of the twelve monthly HICP of the prvious period.

[2] Average maturity 10 years, with the exception of Greece before June 1997 (see footnote 4).

[3] Interest rates: average of the last 12 monthly averages.

[4] Average maturity 10 years from June 1997, 7 years before June 1997.

[5] Debt reduction (-), Debt increase (+)

Tab. A3: Investments in Venture Capital in Europe and the United States (1995)

1995	USA[1]			EU[2]		
	1000 ECU	%	#	1000 ECU	%	#
Total Investment	5748000	+50*	1100 **	5546000	+2	4955
Investment per stage						
Seed and start-up	1476000	26	445	321000	5.7	939
Development	3340000	58		2299000	41	
Leveraged buy-out	932000	16		2926000	53	
Investment per sector						
Information technology	2641000	46		902000	16	
Life Sciences	1398000	24		422000	8	
Non-technology	1709000	30		4222000	76	
Average size of seed capital	932			280		

* 50 % increase in the number of investments (1994-95 period)

** 1100 investments in the United States in 1995

Source: [1] VentureOne (American Company).[2] EVCA.

Fig. A6: Venture Capital

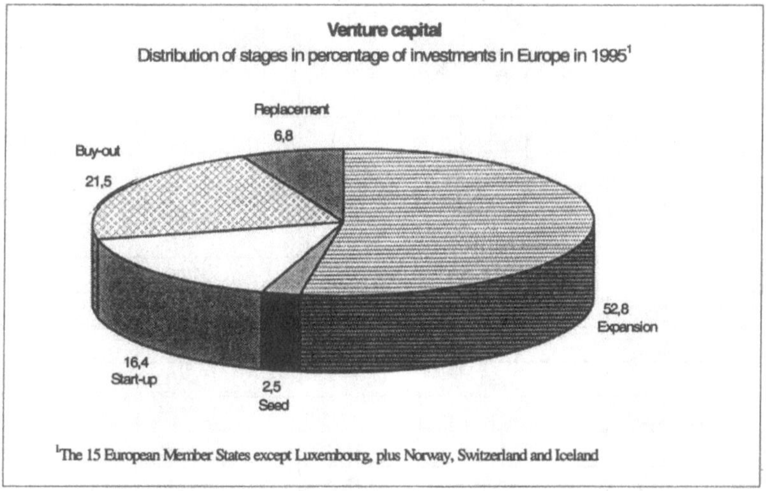

Source: EVCA, Ernst & Young

Fig. A7: Interest Rates in the US and Euroland

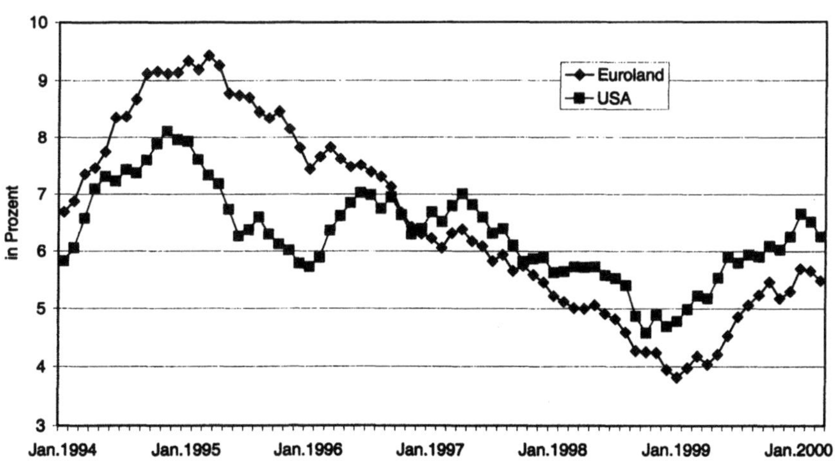

Source: ECB (2000), Monthly Bulletin, May 2000.

Tab. A4: Economic Openness and Diversity of European Countries

	Overall Exports/ GDP (1996)	Extra-Euro Share of exports		Weight in EU GDP (1997)	Weight of PS** in the EU (1998)
		In % of GDP	NA* in % of GDP		
Ireland	70,0	41,8	7,1	1,0	0,65
Belgium-Lux	58,6	23,8	2,8	3,3	1,9
Finland	30,7	21,7	2,6	1,4	0,8
Netherlands	45,2	16,3	1,8	4,6	5,1
Germany	21,8	12,3	1,8	27,6	10,8
Italy	20,7	11,3	1,7	14,1	3,8
Austria	20,5	9,5	1,1	2,7	0,4
France	18,8	9,4	1,3	18,0	7,6
Portugal	22,3	7,8	1,1	1,2	0,4
Spain	17,6	7,0	0,8	6,8	3,7
Greece	7,7	3,9	0,4	1,4	0,5
EMU weighted average	30,4	15,0	2,0	7,8	3,2
Denmark	25,6	14,4	1,2	2,0	1,0
Sweden	33,6	20,5	3,1	2,9	3,3
UK	22,3	11,5	3,0	13,2	20,5
EU average	29,7	15,1	2,1	7,4	4,0

* NA = North America

** Share of Value of Stocks as % of EU-15 GDP

Source: Clausen (2000) and own calculations.

B. Modern Exchange Rate Theory and Schumpetrian Economic Analysis: New Approach and Application to the Euro

1. Introduction

When the Euro and the European Central Bank started the European Currency Union at the beginning of 1999 there were many optimistic observers who anticipated the Euro to quickly become a major rival to the US dollar. Some critics argued that the Euro was bound to be a weak, inflationary currency and that high interest rates would characterize the start of the new currency. Others have argued that the Euro would face problems due to lack of political integration in Euroland. The broader discussion emphasized problems of monetary credibility of the ECB, international currency system issues, potential exchange rate volatility problems and exchange rate misalignment (WELFENS/EICHHORN/PALINKAS, 1998; WELFENS, 1997; 1999a). Recent exchange rate analysis has made some progress but still is fragmented (GÄRTNER, 1993; OBSTFELD/ROGOFF, 1996; TURNOVSKY, 1997).

Given the low inflation rate of 1.1 % in 1999 and of an anticipated 1.5-2% in 2000 and 2001 the main challenge of the Euro in the starting stage certainly is not inflation. Rather, the external value of the Euro which started at 1.1789 US dollar per Euro on January 4, 1999 and fell to below 0.9 by early May 2000 – a depreciation of more than 20% - is the main challenge. Obviously, the Euro has not been successful in convincing international financial markets that it has a medium term potential for an appreciation; nor have central banks outside Europe accumulated high Euro stocks as part of reserve holdings.

While a temporary depreciation is no major problem for economic policy in the EU and Euroland, respectively, a sustained depreciation process would pose complex problems. Inflation might go up as import prices rise strongly. An ongoing depreciation which starts to feed into anticipations of future Euro depreciations also is dangerous in the sense that it will drive up interest rates in Euroland and lead to actual depreciation. A strongly falling Euro could create political tensions in Austria, Germany as well as other Euro zone countries. While there might be some long term factors which would contribute to an appreciation of the Euro the more short-term developments – in the politically critical run-up to 2002 when coins and notes will be introduced – such as the positive transatlantic interest rate differential and high growth in favor of the US do not seem to favor a Euro appreciation.

The following graph shows the development of the Euro against the US-dollar which strongly appreciated in 1999/2000. While the short-term interest rate differential suggests a medium term depreciation of the US-Dollar – based on open interest parity (monthly data) – we observe a medium term appreciation with much short-term volatility. This observed pattern is difficult to explain.

The well-known open interest rate parity puzzle could be explained on the basis of a risk premium R so that $R + i = (^*i + g_e)$, where i is the interest rate, * denotes foreign variable and g_e is the percentage change of the nominal exchange rate. Policymakers in Euroland could try to reduce the risk premium by improving on the decision-making process in economic policy. In a long term triade perspective policymakers face serious problems if interest rate parity and purchasing power parity were not realized since only simultaneous realization of both implies $r=r^*=Y_K=Y_K^*$, respectively. Long term PPP failure would imply that the investment opportunity costs of domestic and foreign investors systematically differ; while we will not look into Japanese problems of unnaturally low real interest rates in the 1990s and associated low investment quality unsolved problems in any major OECD financial system are likely to cause distortions in the whole triade (eg, both US and Euroland stock prices could be overvalued in the sense that much distortionary „carry trade" with Japan– foreigners taking low interest loans in Japan and investing in the US and Euroland – is going on).

Fig. B1: Short-Term Interest Differential (D/K: i^{Euro}-i^{US}) and Growth Rate of Exchange Rate (Euro/$)

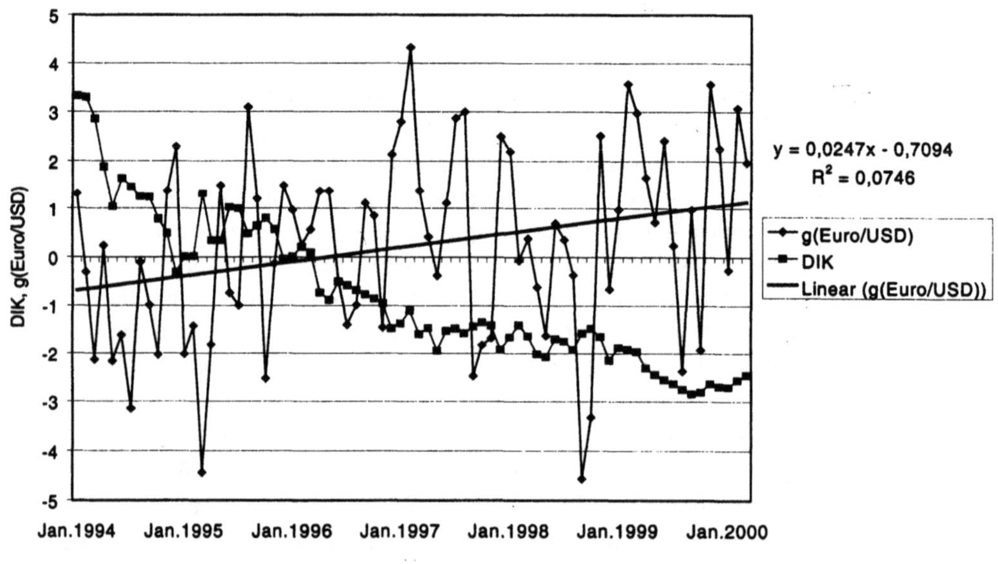

Source: ECB, own calculations

From an economic perspective the Euro depreciation has several effects:

- It stimulates the net exports of goods and services of the Euro area and thus contributes to economic growth in the medium term. However, only about 1/3 of all exports of Germany, France and Italy go to the dollar area. At the same time imported intermediate products become more expensive, which partially impairs exports that are dependent on the heavy usage of such intermediate products.

- It reduces the dollar price of industrial assets in Euroland so that US investors are likely to become more active in Europe, provided that the relative investment climate in the US (and elsewhere) is not improving in an offsetting way. Following FROOT/STEIN (1991) with their imperfect capital market approach we expect that Euroland will benefit from higher FDI inflows relative to GDP, however, this is only a long-term perspective. Moreover, since FROOT/STEIN observed (for the US) that a real devaluation raises FDI inflows relative to GDP it is obvious that raising growth rates in Euroland are likely to be much more important for absolute FDI inflows in the Euro-zone than a depreciation of the Euro.
- It raises doubts about future price stability, and as with increasing import prices, the inflation rate could go over the critical 2 percent margin which in turn is likely to make the ECB raise interest rates.
- It discourages central banks outside Euroland to hold the Euro as a store of value, i.e. to substitute Euro for US dollar in their foreign exchange reserves.
- It could raise Euroland's interest rate beyond the logic of the simple interest parity by generating a currency specific risk premium – similar to what was observed in the 1980s and 1990s for lira denominated bonds, respectively. Market participants will soon have to decide whether the Euro depreciation of 1999/2000 reflects a one term adjustment to a fair market value, a cyclical exchange rate change or a more long term tendency „à la Italienne" implying a long term devaluation bias of the Euro vis-à-vis the US dollar.

On May 8, 2000 the eleven finance ministers from Euro-zone countries made a first joint statement on the new currency. They said they were determined to speed up fiscal consolidation and structural reforms agreed upon at the EU's Lisbon summit in March. It was also indicated that central bank intervention might be considered. The German minister Hans Eichel told journalists that all ministers agree income from selling mobile phone licenses should only be used to reduce public debt. However, there was only weak consensus on this point as the Financial Times noted on its front page on May 9, 2000: „But just as Mr. Eichel´s comments were beginning to make an impression on the market, Mr. Fabius emerged to say there was no general agreement on how to use the income from mobile licenses...ironically, in their separate briefings, Mr. Eichel and Mr. Fabius underlined the need for Euro-11 ministers to speak with one voice to convince markets of the soundness of their policies."

In the following analysis we will present an extended BRANSON model to analyze the fall of the Euro (section 2). Moreover, we will take an analytical look at the impact of debt reduction. By taking into account both the short and the medium term – plus a long term perspective – we can identify the main effects of alternative policies. In section 3 we offer some concluding remarks.

This paper has six motivations:

- We want to include the TOBIN (1958, 1961) risk aspect of portfolio selection, that is take into account that real capital K and real net financial assets A of the private sector are complementary with respect to risk since K and A are subject to rather different risks. We therefore will modify the demand side of the BRANSON exchange rate model in which the demand for asset i is proportionate to A – instead we will use A (K/A) exp z where the parameter z indicates how strong K and A are complementary with respect to risk minimization.
- We want to link the production function and output, respectively, to the BRANSON model and thereby establish a link between the short term and the medium term analysis.
- We will focus on the distinction between government consumption G and government R&D support G′ which raises output and stimulates investment and exports, respectively.
- We want to include foreign direct investment in the goods market and the balance of payments equilibrium
- We finally want to take into account the capacity effect of investment so that we can focus on more long term comparative statics; it will also be shown that a modified Mundell-Fleming model can be displayed in r-lnY-space which could be a natural starting point for analyzing a growth equilibrium
- By emphasizing the relative ratio of the marginal product of capital at home to that abroad, a technology parameter in the production function and research & development we want to incorporate some Schumpeterian aspects into a macro model. By linking some long term aspects with short term asset market dynamics we do not intend to downplay potentially powerful alternative approaches to short term and medium term exchange rate analysis – e.g. the role of rational bubbles or game theoretical analysis in which fundamental analysts and chartist-oriented market players interact. The model setups discussed here are open to various future extensions, including CES production function or a link with various Phillips-curve models or endogenous labor supply and immigration.

Main results are as following: one can usefully combine portfolio analysis and medium and long term goods market and foreign exchange market analysis; the idea of major debt reduction in Germany and France and most other EU countries is supporting the Euro only under certain conditions; it could be that a general debt reduction in Euroland is likely to reinforce the depreciation of the Euro. In the short term a debt reduction will cause an appreciation of the Euro, however, in the long run there will be a depreciation (see Appendix 1 and 4). Reasonable options to stabilize the Euro are launching a series of growth enhancing policy measures, including a supply-oriented fiscal policy, or a high interest rate policy combined with G-7 intervention in currency markets.

In our analysis we focus on links between the short term BRANSON model, the medium term Mundell-Fleming model and the long term purchasing power parity. We highlight the potential divergence between short-term exchange rate changes and long term exchange rate adjustment where our analysis differs from the DORNBUSCH model with its particular overshooting mechanism. It is shown that distinguishing reasons for a rise of (foreign) real interest rates is crucial. We also present a contribution to the theory of optimum currency areas – with arguments in favor of flexible exchange rates within certain limits - where the new argument is that only countries with similar innovation productivity should create a monetary union. In this perspective the 11 Euro starter countries and EU-15, respectively, are not optimal. All the analysis presented allows to better understand the fall of the Euro and the requirements for stabilizing the Euro vis-à-vis the US dollar.

2. Exchange Rate Analysis in the Short and Long Run: A New Approach

As a natural starting point for long term exchange rate analysis we take purchasing power parity in the simple form $eP^*=P$. Assuming money market equilibrium at home, that is $M = M^d$ and money demand $M^d= Pm(Y,i,A)$, and abroad $M^*=M^{d*}$, with $M^{d*} = P^*m^*(Y^*,i^*,A^*)$ we can derive the following equation for the long term exchange rate e'

(1) $e' = (M/M^*)(m^*(Y^*,i^*,A^*)/m(Y,i,A))$

Here M is the money stock, m is real money demand, Y, i, A stand for real output, the nominal interest rate and real financial wealth, respectively;* denotes foreign variables. The partial derivatives m_Y and m_A are positive, m_i is negative. There will be a rise in the exchange rate e', that is a depreciation, if money supply growth in the home country I is higher than abroad. Moreover, assuming identical money demand functions at home and abroad it holds that output growth abroad exceeding that of country I will cause e' to rise; also, a rise of foreign net financial wealth relative to that of country I will raise e'. High Cyclical or structural growthbased on a stock market boom abroad will cause a depreciation of the home currency. In a very simple approach which allows to focus on the short term we specify m and m*, respectively, as follows (e'' is the Euler number):

$$m = Y e''^{-\sigma i} K P^S/P \text{ and } m^* = Y^* e''^{-\sigma^* i^*} K^* P^{*S}/P^*$$

We have restricted financial wealth to the real value of stocks (nominal value equals capital stock K times price index of stocks P^S). The short term exchange rate e then can be modeled on the basis of highly flexible stock prices P^S and P^{*S}, respectively:

(1') $e = (M/M^*) [(Y/Y^*) (K/K^*) (P^S/P^{*S}) (P/P^*) e'' \exp -\sigma(i-i^*)$

For simplicity we have assumed here that $\sigma = \sigma^*$. The following graph shows a high degree of correlation ($r^2 = 0.45$) between the devaluation rate of the Euro vis-à-vis the US Dollar and the growth rate of P^S/P^{*S} (monthly figures of Eurostoxx over S&P-500 index). This could be interpreted as international stock market parity since short term „quasi-arbitrage" requires that the expected domestic return of buying stocks g_{Ps} (percentage change of the stock price index P_s) must be equal to the expected rate of return abroad $g_{Ps^*} + g_e$:

(1") $g_{Ps} = g_{Ps^*} + g_e$

Using expectation values the arbitrage condition implies

(1"') $E(g_{Ps}) = E(g_{Ps^*}) + E(g_e)$

From a theoretical perspective it would be important to have a theory which explains to which extent the exchange rate affects the stock price at home (country I) and abroad (country II), and which link between stock prices and the exchange rate exist; in a stationary equilibrium with foreign direct investment abroad – with a share χ of K^* owned by firms from country I – and foreign investment in country I – with a share χ^{**} of K owned by firms from country II – a straightword function in a world with Cobb-Douglas production function $Y = K \exp ß\ L \exp 1-ß$ (symetrically for country II) and infinitely lived capital stock would be:

(1.1) $P^s = (1-\chi^{**})ßPY/r + e\chi ß^*P^*Y^*/r$

Here the stock price of country I firm is the discounted future profits from ownership of the home capital stock plus the foreign capital stock. If there is underutilization of the capital stock a depreciation —a rise of e – would stimulate net exports and therefore raise Y, it also would raise profits accruing from abroad; while a depreciation will dampen Y^* the net effect nevertheless could be a rise of the overall share price. To the extent that short term interest rate parity holds in the form real interest rate $r = r^* + [e^E/e] - 1$ a rise of e, assuming an exogenous expected exchange rate e^E – will reduce r which dampens the rise of Ps. An exogenous rise of the share price could stimulate consumption demand if this includes a wealth effect and thereby it would reduce net exports of goods and services for any given potential output so that the exchange rate would fall – assuming given net capital outflows. Similarily to (1"") the foreign stock price is $P^{s*} = (1-\chi)ß^*P^*Y^*/r^* + (1/e)\chi^{**}ßPY/r^*$. Again we could develop a similar reasoning for the link between e and Ps* and vice versa. In a more general approach we could state the hypothesis that

(1.2) $P^s=P^s(Y,Y^*,r,e,Z)$

where Z is the number of patent applications; an alternative could be the R&D capital stock which recently has been incorporated in the Pantha Rhei III macro model (MEYER/WELFENS, 1999) which shows an output multiplier for an increase in the research and development stock of about five times that for goverment consumption expenditures.

As regards long term stock price development there has indeed been emphasis in recent theoretical and empirical research that firms' expenditures on R&D and other intangible assets, including internet activities, positively have influenced stock market valuation (HALL, 1999; DARBY/LIU/ZUCKER, 1999; DESMET et al., 2000). In a Schumpetrian perspective increasing innovation dynamics will raise stock market prices. The increasing global leadership of US firms in patent applications and in the use of the internet in 1999/2000 thus could explain the relative rise of the US stock price; this will lead to a depreciation of the Euro, where one will observe an overshooting effect. Similarly, a rise of Euroland output relative to the US would cause an appreciation of the Euro in the long run – an overshooting effect will, however, to an adjustment path governed by stock market parity (equation 1'').

A specific weakness of Euroland could be that, according to findings of MUELLER/YURTOGLU (2000) German, French and Italian firms quoted on national stock markets tend to have inefficient investment decisions for projects financed from cash flows: dividend payments are found to be relatively low in these – and some other European – countries, overinvestment and insufficient return on investment seems to be a problem of the core of Euroland; according to MUELLER/YURTOGLU neither the UK nor Sweden nor the US show similar problems who argue that bank dominated financial systems tend to contribute to inefficient investment financing. From this perspective it would be important that Euroland's core countries politically favor the use of stock markets as a channel of financing investment. This implies that the Euro not only suffers from much discussed labor market inflexibilities in various countries of the Euro zone but equally from capital market problems.

Taking into account (1') and emphasizing that Y,Y*, K, K*, P, P* are slow variables in a macroeconomic system in which the money markets always are in equilibrium one could estimate a short term exchange rate equation $\ln e = \ln e_{t-1} + a_2 \ln P^s/P^{*s} + a_3\sigma i + a_4\sigma^* i^*$; based on first differences such an approach indeed is shown in the appendix 5 – with good out-of-sample forecast results. The interaction of asset markets and goods markets deserves more attention in future research. This holds not least because the long term ratio of assets to GDP is increasing in OECD countries which implies that wealth or asset effects increasingly will affect investment and consumption.

Fig. B2: Growth of the Ratio Between the Stock Market Indices Eurostoxx and Standard & Poor and Growth Rate of Exchange Rate (Euro/$)

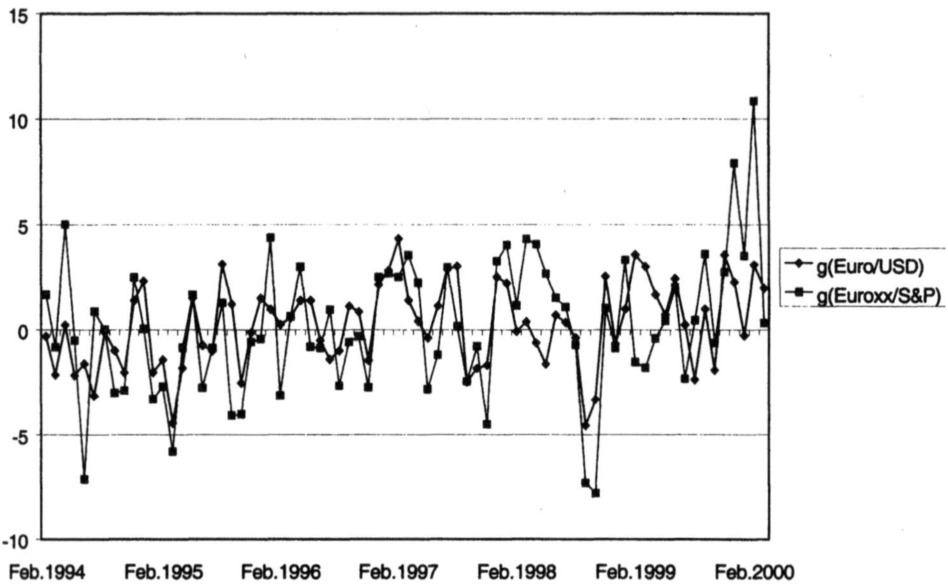

Source: ECB, own calculations

We now return to equation (1) and will define financial wealth as not including stocks so that we follow the Branson model. If the interest rate abroad is rising more slowly (or falling faster) than in country I the long-term exchange rate will increase according to (1). This, however, is not what the short term analysis based on portfolio theoretical approaches would suggest: it holds that, in particular, a rise of the short term interest rate abroad will cause the exchange rate to rise as can be shown in the simple BRANSON model with money market, domestic bond market and foreign bond market where MM, BB and F*F* represent the respective equilibrium conditions, that is equations 2a,b,c. The MM curve has a positive slope since a rise of the exchange rate (depreciation) will raise nominal wealth and therefore the demand for money; the excess demand in the money market will be eliminated if i rises adequately. A similar reasoning applies to the BB curve. The F*F* curve has a negative slope since a rise of e causes an excess supply due to the increase of (eF*) while demand rises underproportionately This excess supply is eliminated if i is falling adequately. While the left hand side shows supply in the respective market the right hand represents asset demand where the desired share in each asset is proportionate to nominal wealth A′. Note that a is the exogenous expected depreciation rate.

(2a)	$M = n(i,i^*,a)A'$;	money market equilibrium
(2b)	$B = b(i,i^*,a)A'$	bonds market equilibrium
(2c)	$eF^* = f(i,i^*,a)A'$	foreign bond market equilibrium

Fig. B3: Portfolio Equilibrium in the Simple Branson Model

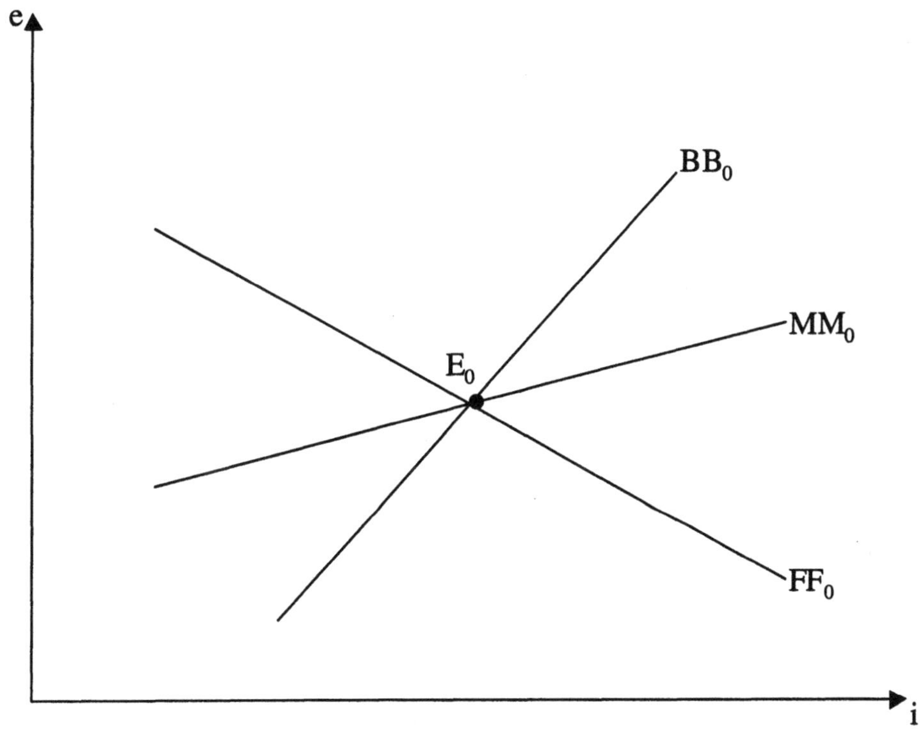

Since the budget constraint is $A' = M + B + eF^*$ only two of the above equations are independent so that in e-i-space the intersection of the BB curve and the F*F* curve determines the equilibrium (an alternative could be the intersection of MM and F*F*). The simplest way to take into account the goods market is to impose the profit maximizing condition $Y_K = r$ – where Y_K is the marginal product of capital – while assuming that there is no inflation initially so that the nominal interest rate $i=r$ at home and $i^*=r^*$ abroad. What happens if the exogenous variable i^* is increasing or if the expected depreciation is rising? The BB-curve shifts to the right while the F*F* curve shifts upwards: The result is a depreciation while the interest rate could rise (strong rightward shift of BB as with BB_1 in Fig. 2) or fall (small rightward shift of BB as with BB_2). The latter is unlikely unless the demand for domestic bonds reacts very strongly to a rise of i* or the expected depreciation rate a. An increase in the foreign marginal product will feed into the model via an increase of r*.

Applying this reasoning to the Euro in 1999/2000.I the depreciation of the Euro could be explained by the direct rise of the nominal US interest rate or by indirect effect of a rise of the marginal product of capital abroad. An alternative explanation is a rise in the expected depreciation rate brought about by political changes.

Fig. B4: Rise of Expected Devaluation Rate and of Foreign Interest Rate

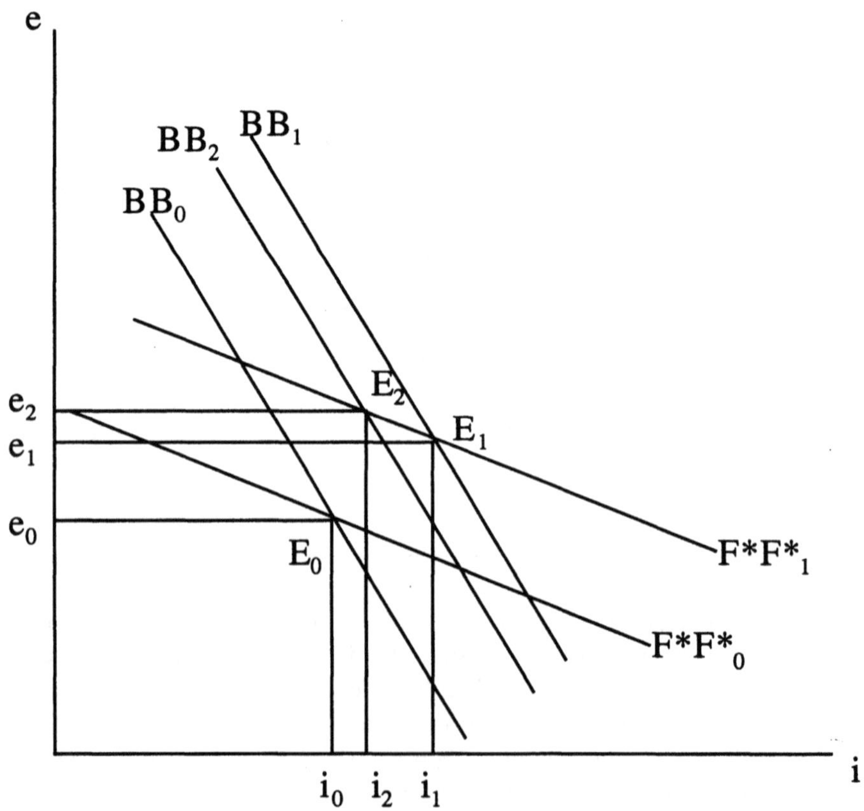

2.1. Optimum Exchange Rate Flexibility and Optimum Currency Area

With respect to the issue of exchange rate volatility and flexibility, respectively, it is important to understand that the short term BRANSON model and the long-term equilibrium equation (1) have contrasting implications for exchange rate changes, and in some cases the contrast is modest, in other cases stark. In the following graph we display in panel a) the interest rate parity line IP – summarizing the domestic and foreign bonds market implicitly - which is based on interest rate parity $i = i^* + (e^E - e)/e$. The expected exchange rate e^E could be determined by adaptive expectations – or other forms of learning – in the medium run, but in the long run it must be consistent with purchasing power parity, that is equation 1, if there is to be a general equilibrium. For the short run and the immediate impact round we will assume that the expected devaluation rate $a = (e^E - e)/e$ is not changing at all.

To highlight the different implications of the (modified) BRANSON model and equation (1) we will consider a rise of the foreign real interest rate r* where we assume that there is no inflation at home and abroad so that i=r and i*=r*. The rise of the foreign real interest rate will shift the IP line upwards (IP_1) so the intersection of the new money market equilibrium line MM_1 in point E''_1 indicates an interest rate rise and a currency depreciation. Note that the MM curve has shifted upwards since the rise of r* implies a rise of the opportunity cost of holding money abroad and at home (reducing the demand for money) so that a higher financial wealth and hence a rise of the exchange rate is required to raise demand for money and to restore equilibrium in the i money market, respectively. The relevant equilibrium condition is $M/P = n(i,i^*, a, Y)A$ where A is real financial wealth $(eF^*+B+M)/P$. We have modified the real demand for money in the BRANSON model in the sense that we added real output Y as an argument, and this will be explained in more detail subsequently. Here it suffices to point out that in principle this specification chosen is consistent with that in equation (1).

Fig. B5: Short-Term Exchange Rate Reaction versus Long Term Exchange Rate Adjustment

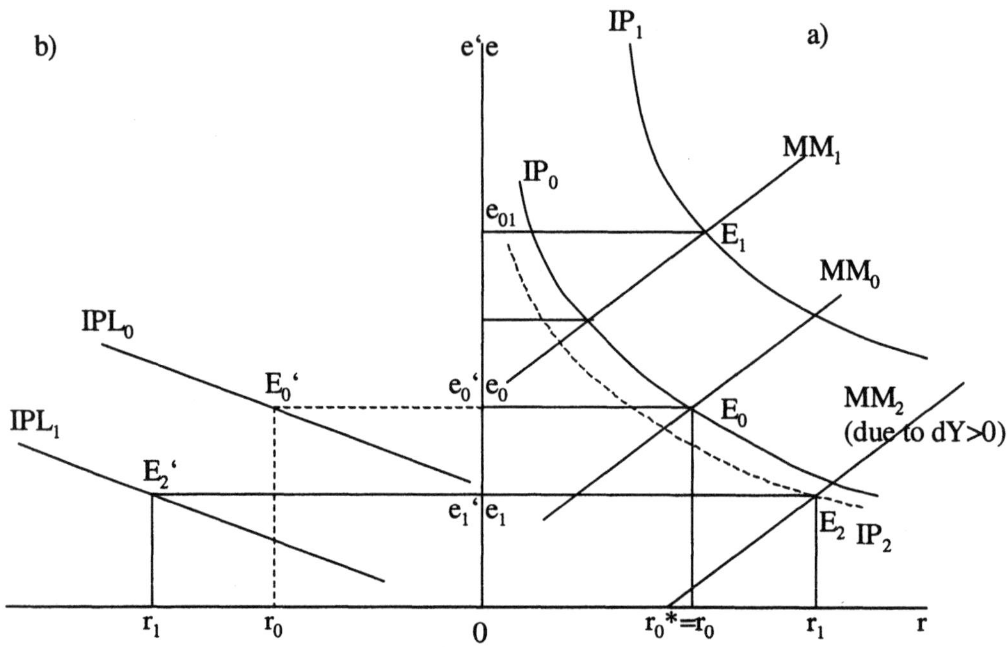

In panel b) we show equation (1) which in e´-r-space is an upward-sloping curve IPL. The rise of the foreign real interest rate will cause – assuming for the moment that Y* and Y will not be affected – a downward shift of the IPL line (IPL_1) so that there is a large divergence between the short term exchange rate e_{01} and the implied long run rate e'_1. The larger the divergence the more difficult would it be to switch from a system of flexible exchange rates to a regime of fixed exchange rates - artificially fixing the exchange rate would lead to a fast and much stronger rise of the domestic interest rate as rising net capital outflows will cause an excess demand in the currency market with following exchange market intervention of the central bank which thereby is raising the money supply. However, this does not imply that full exchange rate flexibility is always the best solution. High exchange rate volatility comes at a cost, e.g. there is empirical evidence that high exchange rate volatility reduces domestic investment (WELFENS/JUNGMITTAG, 1997) and foreign direct investment (UNCTAD, 1993); indeed depending on elasticities of the respective asset demand functions and the functions in the goods – and labor – markets there will be an optimum degree of exchange rate flexibility, that is a corridor around e_o. and the respective real exchange rate.

In a system of flexible exchange rates a reconciliation between the (modified) BRANSON model and purchasing power parity can be achieved only if the expected exchange rate at some point of time – in the medium term – is governed by equation (1) or a variation of it; e.g. we could stipulate that for market participants in assets markets it will hold that $e^E = P/P^* = M/[P^* \, m(Y,i,A)]$ where i is, of course, influenced by the foreign interest rate i*. Even if the foreign price level is exogenous and constant the cross-border interest link must be taken into account. Panel a) shows that the long term equilibrium – with constant Y and Y* and A and A* - is point I. In panel b) the adjustment of the expected exchange rate will have to shift down the IP-line downwards in a consistent manner.

However, taking a look at the long run we must take into account the impact of the rise of r* on foreign real output Y* and other variables abroad and in country I. It is immediately clear that we must distinguish between

- (i) a rise of r due to a higher supply of foreign bonds abroad (dB*>0 which will not affect F*, the part held by residents in country I as long as this country has no current account surplus),
- (ii) a rise in the central bank rate r'^*;
- (iii) an increase in the marginal product of capital Y^*_K.

Taking a look at case (i) there will be an upward shift in the interest parity line, that is the move from IP_0 to IP_1. If the rise of r* dampens output abroad so that Y* would fall, the long term implication in accordance with equation (1) is an appreciation since m* and m*/m, respectively, are both reduced because of a higher interest rate and because of a reduced output Y*. Since this fall of Y* will reduce imports in country II so that exports of country I will be reduced which in turn reduce Y, the overall impact clearly is a reduction of m*/m so that the IPL line is shifted downwards (IPL_1 instead of IPL_0). Thus, while the short-term impact is depreciation, the long-term impact is an appreciation. To get a consistent solution in panel b) and a) it must be assumed that at some point – in the medium term – exchange rate expectation is adjusting towards a lower e^E which shifts the IP curve downwards and we get the intersection point E_2 in panel a) which corresponds to E'_2 in panel b).

Now we turn to case (ii) and (iii), respectively. It makes a difference whether the rise of r* was brought about by central bank action, namely a reduction of M*, or by a positive productivity shock in an environment of profit maximization, a rise of Y^*_K which must be equal to r* where for the moment we ignore any risk premium; in principle the following reasoning applies mutatis mutandis to a relative rise of Y^*_K / Y_K which would be caused by a relative improvement in foreign innovation dynamics. From this perspective it is clear that the optimum exchange rate literature can be enriched by an additional criterion, namely that countries potentially willing to create a monetary union should have a similar rate of innovativeness so that no large relative changes (Y^*_K/Y_K) are to be expected.

Fig. B6: Innovation Clusters in the EU (patent applications per 1 Mio inhabitants)

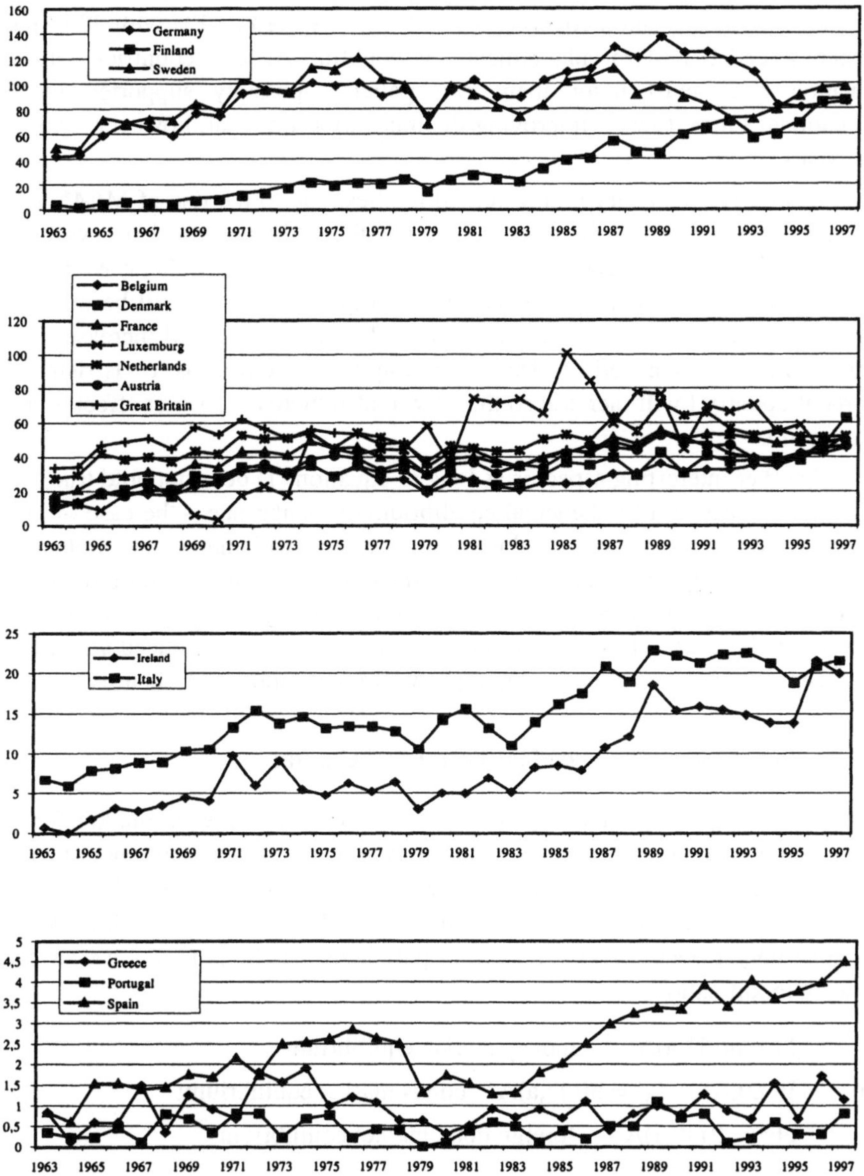

Source: JUNGMITTAG (2000)

Comparing EU countries one indeed finds that most Southern countries (Greece, Portugal and Spain) are in the same cluster of innovativeness as measured by innovations per number of inhabitants, that is patent applications per 1 Mio. inhabitants. JUNGMITTAG (2000) identifies four group of innovators in the EU-15 group where two weaker groups show relatively low innovation rates, and from this perspective monetary union covering the full EU – or even an EU with 20 or more members after EU eastern enlargement – is doubtful. At least countries with low innovation rates must tailor their own policies, possibly supported by EU supranational funds, toward improving the innovation rate that, however, will take many years.

Restrictive monetary policy abroad implies, due to the rise of M/M*, a rise of e´ in equation (1) unless the money demand effect – the fall of m*/m – will show a more than offsetting effect. If there is a positive productivity shock we will see that investment $I^*(r^*, Y_K^*, ...)$ is increasing so output and profits will be increased. Higher profits also imply a rise of A*. Money demand abroad will increase so that m*/m – with a constant ratio M/M* - drives up e´. Moreover, as Y* is rising, net exports of country I will increase so that Y will also increase, the net effect is still a rise of m*/m.

Another interesting aspect is as long as equation (1) does not hold true, trade will not take place at a fundamental equilibrium exchange rate – the case of „false trading" - and this trade and the induced output effects will change the fundamental equilibrium exchange rate consistent with equation (1). From a welfare theoretical aspect it should be analyzed by how much „false trading" and high exchange rate volatility, in the sense of the initial ratio $e_{01}/e'1$, – and further induced volatility in the adjustment process – impairs output growth or undermines job security.

2.2. Changes in Domestic Marginal Product of Capital

As a next step we will implicitly take into account the domestic market for real capital, and we will assume an exogenous change in the marginal product of capital in country I. Assuming that firms will invest more in this situation and that part of investment is financed by additional corporate bonds (B2) which are lumped here with government bonds (B1) – reflecting past budget deficits G-T - we have the following modification:

(2a) $M = n(i,i^*,a)A'$; money market equilibrium

(2b) $B(\Sigma(G\text{-}T), Y_K) = b(i,i^*,a)A'$ bonds market equilibrium;

(2c) $eF^* = f(i,i^*,a)A'$ foreign bond market equilibrium

(2d) $M + B + eF^* = A'$

In this model, setting a rise in the domestic marginal product of capital will lead to an upward shift of the BB curve and therefore raise the exchange rate and the interest rate. The increase in the marginal product of capital thus raises the interest rate and causes a currency depreciation. The above specification can be modified in order to take into account the portfolio-theoretical argument that the ratio K/(A'/P) would positively influence the demand for money and bonds – due to the desire to minimize the portfolio risk: K and real financial wealth are complementary. We therefore replace in a modified equation 2a) A' by A (K/A)exp. z, we also restate the left-hand side as M/P so that the equilibrium conditions refers to real money balances.

Furthermore we can use a Cobb-Douglas-function for output Y = V(1-u) K exp. ß L exp. (1-ß), where V is a technology parameter, u is the unemployment rate, K real capital, L labor and ß the output elasticity of capital. Thus, we can replace K by Y exp. 1/ß [V (1-u)] exp. -1/ß L exp. - (1-ß)/ß.

We respecify the demand for money as M^d/P = n(...) Y exp z/ß (A exp 1-z) [(V (1-u)) exp -z/ß][L exp -(1-ß) z/ß], where A is real financial wealth; the supply side is now in real terms, that is M/P for equation (3a). Similarly, the other demand functions have to be respecified. Note that this specification takes into account the portfolio theoretical analysis of TOBIN who has argued that with respect to risk net real financial wealth and real capital are complementary. The systems 3a, b, c now combine a short-term portfolio model with flexible interest rate plus exchange rate and sticky output and price level which only reacts in the medium term.

(3a) M/P= n(i,i*,a) (Y exp z/ß) [A exp (1-z)] [(V (1-u)) exp -z/ß][L exp -(1-ß) z/ß]

(3b) B/P(Σ(G-T), Y_K)= b(i,i*,a) Y exp z/ß A exp (1-z) [(V (1-u)) exp -z/ß][L exp -(1-ß) z/ß]

(3c) eF*/P = f(i,i*,a) Y exp z/ß A exp (1-z) [(V (1-u)) exp -z/ß][L exp -(1-ß) z/ß]

To the extent that one only interested in the impact of Y (or K) and A we could impose for simplicity normalizations of the technical parameter V and labor L to unity. Assuming furthermore that unemployment u = 0, expressions within the last two square brackets can be dropped from eq. (3a) - (3c).

An increase in the domestic marginal product of capital will rise at given K output in the medium term and thus the demand for money, bonds and foreign bonds in real terms. However, it also will raise in the short term the real bonds supply (BB_1) as firms will finance part of their additional investments by corporate bonds; note that we have assumed no inflation so that the graph is shown in e-r-space An interesting application could be the internet and mobile telephone boom based on considerable technological progress. In our model the internet boom thus translates into a higher marginal product of capital.

In the short run we thus assume that output is not reacting, so that the BB curve will shift to the right much more than in the medium term – once output has increased. The short-term reaction, a rise in the marginal product of capital, is thus a large currency depreciation while the medium term could be a modest depreciation of the currency.

Special Case: Interest Rate Parity

A simplified version of the above model holds with interest rate parity. In e-i-space the interest rate parity line (IP) is downward sloping. The money market equilibrium is upward sloping. We assume no inflation at home and abroad, in addition we impose the profit maximization condition:

(3d) $r = Y_K - R(A/K)$

where R is the risk premium for holding real capital; instead of the ratio A/K we also could use A/Y if the production function is Cobb-Douglas and the population constant. In the lower part of the following graph we have the marginal product of capital as a function of K, so that we can determine e-r in the upper part of the diagram and the marginal product of capital Y_K in the lower part; note that in point F it holds $r = Y_K$, that is we have no risk premium on investment in machinery and equipment. Additionally we have output as the integral under the Y_K-curve, that is the area OAE'N (labor income is equal to triangle AE'F). If domestic marginal product is rising due to a technology shift output will increase in accordance with E''.

As (A/K) falls there is now a positive risk premium so that the real interest rate ri is smaller than the marginal product of capital. The fall of A/K – implying that (Y/A) will rise – will shift the MM-curve downwards (MM1) so that point G is the new equilibrium. Assuming that market participants will adjust their expected exchange rate e^E downwards in line with equation (1) as they anticipate a rise of Y we will have a downward shift of the IP1 line: Since r* has not changed expectations we must adjust until we have $r = r^* + a$, where a is zero (point H).

Fig. B7: Interest Rate Parity, Money Market Equilibrium and Output

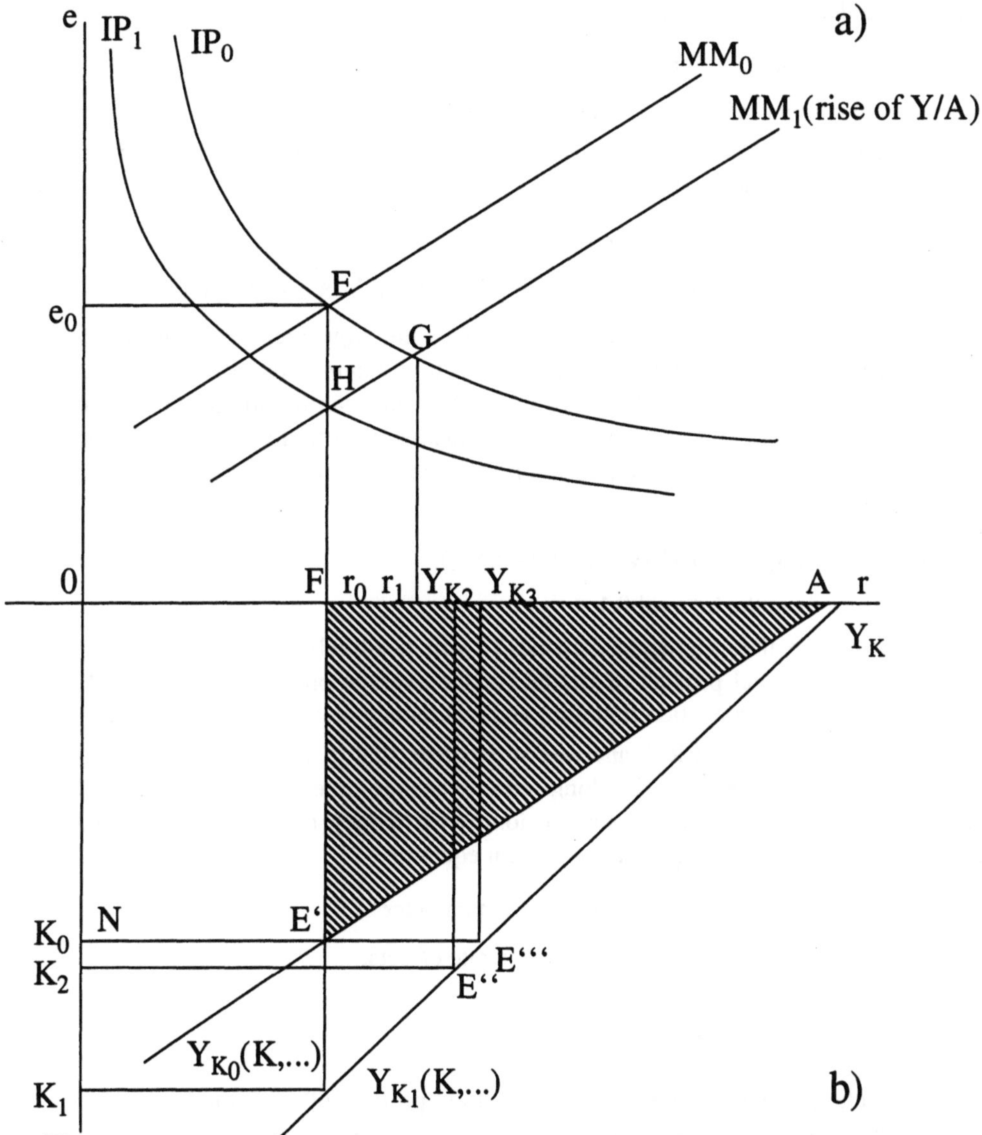

General Adjustment Perspective

Assuming that the demand for money will adjust with a time lag we can state (suppressing the time index for contemporaneous variables):

$\ln m = h(\ln m^D - \ln m_{t-1}) + \ln m_{t-1},$

where the adjustment factor h is in the interval 0,1.

Inserting the money demand function we have the following specification which can be tested empirically:

(5) $\ln m = h \ln m^d + (1-h) \ln m_{t-1}$

(5.1) $\ln m = h \ln n(i,i^*,a) + hz/ß \ln Y + h(1-z) \ln A + (1-h) \ln m_{t-1}$

With respect to output we assume the following adjustment equation which stipulates an adjustment proportionate to Y^d-Y_{t-1}. It is assumed that the adjustment is faster if innovation activities are high while the latter can be proxied by patent applications Z. Moreover, we assume that the adjustment coefficient depends on the Tobin $q = P^K/P$ positively, but negatively on the real interest rate r and the unemployment rate.

$\ln Y - \ln Y_{t-1} = v'(Z,q,r,u)(\ln Y^d (w,m,Y/K) - \ln Y_{t-1}),$

where v' is in the interval 0,1.

We assume that aggregate demand Y^d will positively depend on the real wage rate, the marginal product of capital (or the average product of capital Y/K under Cobb-Douglas production function) and real money balances, respectively.

In regards to empirical analysis it is clear that a two-stage estimation procedure must be applied. The long-term exchange rate can be determined according to equation (1) where we use long term money demand at home and abroad. If we use the exchange rate adjustment equation

$e - e_{t-1} = s'(e' - e_{t-1})$; where s' is an adjustment parameter

we can model the short-term exchange rate effects.

2.3. Debt Reduction Policy

A debt reduction policy financed with windfall tax profits will shift the MM curve upwards ($MM_{0'}$) as the ratio K/A increases. However, in order to minimize portfolio risk, the initial K/A will be restored meaning investment demand will fall. Debt reduction will shift the BB curve to the left (BB_1) but as output is falling due to reduced investment the BB curve will shift to the right. The result is a depreciation. At this reduced exchange rate there will be higher net exports of goods and services so that the "Branson-exchange rate" feeds into the goods market

(IS-LM-ZZ-model). The IS-LM-ZZ-model in turn – in particular a change of output – will feed into the modified Branson-model as the ratio Y/A has changed. Note also that the immediate impact of a domestic debt reduction could be a rising demand for foreign bonds, raising e, until the rise of eF* has compensated for the reduction of B; that is K/A has been restored to the initial intermediate level – a potential depreciation is at E'_0. In the appendix we show that a positive system determinant brings about the short-term result: de/(-dB) < 0, but long run results are different.

Fig. B8: Debt Reduction Policy in a Modified Branson Model

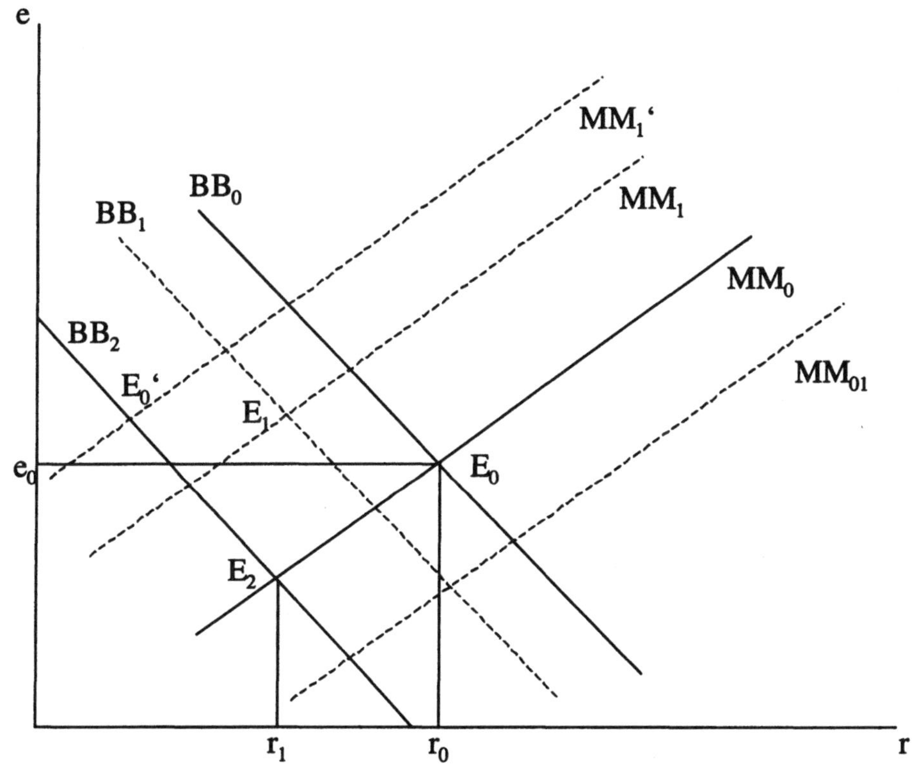

2.4. Government Budget Constraint in a Supply-side Framework

We assume that government has expenditures for public consumption G and for support of research and development (G') and interest rate payments. Revenues are from issuing public bonds (B1), seigniorage and from income taxes T(Y). Thus the government budget constraint is given by

(6) $G+G'+iB_1/P - T(Y) = (dB_1/dt)/P + (dM/dt)/P$

Government instruments are government consumption G, government support G′ for research and development and the tax rate, T_Y. Monetary policy will determine M. One can also take into account a link between accumulated government R&D support, where V in the production function could be proportionate to past R&D support. Interestingly, the Pantha rhei III model (MEYER/WELFENS, 1999) shows a much higher output multiplier for an increase in the economy's stock of R&D than in the case of an exogenous increase of investment.

The stock-flow adjustment in this model is based on four equations, namely the balance of payments constraint, the government budget constraint, the money market adjustment equation and the output market adjustment equation. In regardsto the current account the constraint is given by:

(7) $dF^*/dt = PX - eP^*X^*$

where X and X* are exports and imports, respectively.

2.5. A Portfolio-Augmented Mundell-Fleming Model

An interesting model exercise is to combine our modified portfolio model with the Mundell Fleming world where we will use the balance of payments equilibrium condition and the goods market equilibrium condition in combination with our portfolio sub-model. We will assume that $X=x(...)Y^*$ while imports $X^* = x^*(...)Y$. Regarding the balance of payments constraint for simplicity we will later use a modified form of equation (7) which is as follows:

(7′) $dF^*/dt = \varepsilon\ (Px(q^*,...)Y^*/[eP^*x^*(q^*...)Y])$,

where q* is the real exchange rate eP^*/P and the parameter $\varepsilon>0$

Note that we have used the familiar export function $X = x(q^*,...)Y^*$ and the import function $X^* = x^*(q^*...)Y$. The reason for using this formulation is that we want to derive a convenient system of equations which combine the balance of payments constraint (and the goods market equilibrium condition) with the portfolio system: basically in r-lnY-space.

A long term equilibrium condition must combine equation (7´) and (3a) where a straightforward specification – with e" representing the Euler number and σ representing positive elasticities- is for (3a)

(3a´) M/P= {(Y exp z/ß) [A exp (1-z)] [(V (1-u)) exp -z/ß][L exp -(1-ß) z/ß]} e"exp $-\sigma_1 i - \sigma_2(i^*+a)$

Similarly we can specify for equation (3b´)

(3b´) B/P = {(Y exp z/ß) [A exp (1-z)] [(V (1-u)) exp -z/ß][L exp -(1-ß) z/ß]} e"exp $\sigma_3 i/(i^*+a)$

and

(3c´) eF*/P = {(Y exp z/ß) [A exp (1-z)] [(V (1-u)) exp -z/ß][L exp -(1-ß) z/ß]} e"exp $-\sigma_4 i/(i^*+a)$

It is convenient to divide (7´) – taking into account the export and import function, respectively - by equation (3c´) to obtain:

(3c") (dF*/dt)/F* =
ε (x(q*...)Y*/{[P*x*(q*...) [Y exp (1+z/ß)] [A exp (1-z)] [(V (1-u)) exp -z/ß]
[L exp -(1-ß) z/ß] e"exp $-\sigma_4 i/(i^*+a)$ }

This equation reflects the balance of payments equilibrium line (ZZL) in our modified MUNDELL-FLEMING model. One may note: Since this equation contains the unemployment rate we could link it to a Phillips-type sub-model for the labor market to analyze medium-term adjustment.

In principle there are two possible statements of a long term external equilibrium condition: (I) we can set dF*/dt =0 and then obtain after taking logarithms:

(3c"´) ε´ + x´(q*...) +y* = p* +x*´$-\sigma_4 i/(i^*+a)$ + (1+z/ß)y -(1-z)a´ -(z/ß)(v-u) - [(1-ß)z/ß]lnL

where lnε = ε´, lnx=x´, lnx*=x*´, lnP*=p*, ln A=a´, lnY =y and lnY*=y*.

The present model setup does not integrate foreign direct investment. A convenient way to do this is to modify the investment-output function by taking into account that the terms of trade have an influence of foreign direct investment; FROOT/STEIN (1991) have shown theoretically and empirically that a real depreciation of the currency will stimulate FDI inflows relative to GDP. Hence j = j(r,q*,G´, Y_K/Y_K^*) where the partial derivative of j with respect to q* is positive; it has been assumed that FDI inflows also depend on G‘ and the ratio of the domestic marginal product of capital to the foreign marginal product of capital.

We also have to take into account that the equilibrium condition for the foreign exchange market must be modified. If there are only portfolio flows the equilibrium condition for the foreign exchange market can be written as:

$$(PX/eP^*X) = \{(\{(Y \exp z/ß) [A \exp (1-z)] [(V (1-u)) \exp -z/ß][L \exp -(1-ß) z/ß]\} e'' \exp -\sigma_4 i/(i^*+a)\}/(eF^*/P)$$

The left hand side represents the excess supply from the trade balance, while the right-hand side is the ratio of the demand for foreign bonds relative to supply – indicating the degree of excess demand for capital balance transactions. With (net) FDI inflows we require as a balance of payments equilibrium condition that

(3c"") $[PX/(eP^*X)](1+ \psi(q^*,G', Y_K/Y_K^*)= \{\{...\}\}$

where the variable ψ is positive and is a proxy for FDI inflows which, besides the influence of q* and the ratio of domestic to foreign marginal product will depend on government R&D support; here we assume that multinational investment is mainly occuring in sectors which are technology intensive – a rather realistic assumption. An exogenous increase of the foreign marginal product of capital will reduce j and thus shift the ISL curve to the left, moreover it will require higher portfolio capital inflows for any given trade balance deficit so that the ZZL curve will shift upwards. It is important to recognize that the reduction of j will reduce the increase in the production potential and thus could induce market participants to anticipate lower future economic growth and lower future current account surplus positions – both elements which could raise the expected exchange rate. We do not want to look into the issue of exchange rate expectation in detail, suffice to say that if demand and supply functions in the foreign exchange markets include, besides e, a speculative element in the sense that the first and second derivative are considered by market participantsand one easily can show the possibility of dynamic instability (CHIANG, 1984, chapter 15).

Interestingly, a debt reduction policy which reduces real financial wealth A and a′, respectively, will shift the ZZL curve upwards in r-Y space. In r-y-space the slope of ZZL – our equilibrium line for the foreign exchange market - is positive. Compared to the standard Mundell Fleming model we can see here that the output elasticity ß and the "Tobin risk coefficient" z play a role. The more complementary K and real financial wealth A are from the perspective of portfolio risk minimization – that is the higher z – the steeper the ZZL-curve will be; the larger ß, the more flat the ZZL curve will be. It also is obvious that the standard balance of payments equilibrium curve implicitly assumes that wealth – here lnA – is constant.

(II) The alternative for stating a long term equilibrium condition is to assume the case of a growing economy: there is a desired ratio (eF*/P)/Y which for an equilibrium exchange rate would require a constant ratio (F*/P)/Y. A full long term equilibrium would also require that the unemployment rate u be zero.

The familiar goods market (equilibrium) condition will be stated slightly different than usual where C is consumption, I investment, G government consumption, G′ government R&D support, X and X* exports and imports, respectively:

(7.1) $Y = C(..) + I(...) + G + G' + X\text{-}q^*X^*$

Assuming that $C = c(...)Y$ and $I = j(...)Y$ and export and import functions, namely $X = x(...)Y^*$ and $X^* = x^*(...)Y$ we can rewrite (7") as follows:

(7.1′) $Y[1\text{-}c(...) - j(...) - \gamma - \gamma' + q^*x^*(...)] = x(...)Y^*$

where γ=G/Y and γ'=G′/Y.

Using the approximation ln (1+small number) = small number we can easily logarithmize the goods market equilibrium condition (7") and obtain an equation which is a semilogarithmic IS-curve in r-lnY space:

(7.1") $y - c(r, \tau, \tau^E...) - j(r, \gamma'..) - \gamma - \gamma' + q^*x^*(q^*...) = x'(q^*,\gamma'...) + y^*$

where y=ln Y, y*=lnY*, j=I/Y, $\delta c/\delta a' > 0$ (standard), $\delta c/\delta \tau^E < 0$ $\delta j/\delta r < 0$, $\delta j/\delta \gamma' > 0$ $\delta x'/\delta \gamma' > 0$

The ISL curve which portrays the aggregate demand side is the familiar IS curve. The advantage in r-lnY-space is that in comparative statistics analysis we can easily recognize how large the growth rate is. Since we use a linear-homogeneous production function and assume the marginal product rule with respect to production factors holds we have

(7.2) $Y = rK + wL$

(7.2′) $Y = rK + (1\text{-}ß)Y$

Consequently the increase in output – that is supply - is

(7.3) $ßdY/dt = rI + Kdr/dt$

If the interest rate is constant we can divide by Y and ß on both sides and come up with:

(7.3′) $dy = r(I/Y)/ß$

In the following figure which shows given real interest rate – say due to perfectly elastic international capital flows – a rightward shift in the ISL curve as a consequence of increased government consumption we can determine whether thereis really a new long term equilibrium where long term means that we take into account the capacity effect of investment. The new demand determined y is $y_1$instead of the initial y_0. The tangens μ shows dy/r=j/ß so that we have a long term equilibrium only if the new production potential is given by point F which is identical to y_1. If point F, the new production potential, were to the right of y_1 (point

F') there would be an excess supply so that point E_1 cannot be a long term equilibrium.

Fig. B9: True Equilibrium in Supply-Augmented Macro Model

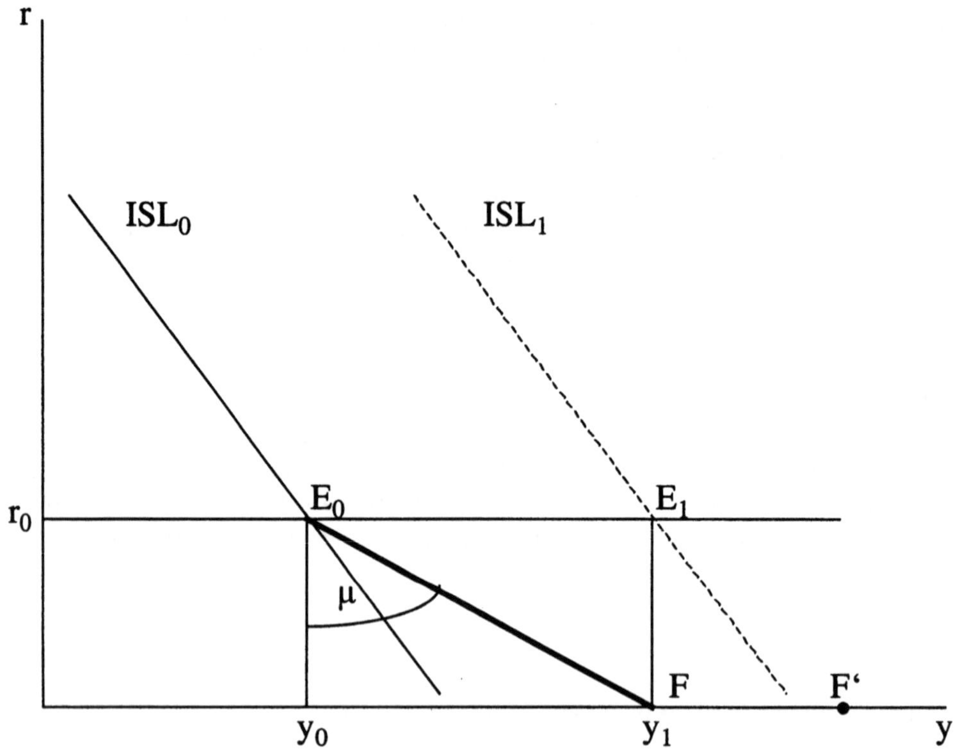

We can combine equation (7.3´) with (7.1") to derive a simple differential equation for the situation of a constant real interest rate in y, namely by replacing j in equation (7.3´) from (7.1):

(7.3") $dy = (r/ß)y - (r/ß)[c(r...) + \gamma + \gamma' - q^*x^*(q^*...) + x'(q^*,\gamma'...) + y^*]$

This non-homogenous differential equation can be easily solved for the case of exogenous or equilibrium terms of trade q*:

(7.3"´) $dy = \Omega\, e'' \exp -(r/ß)t - [c(r...) + \gamma + \gamma' - q^*x^*(q^*...) + x'(q^*,\gamma'...) + y^*]$

From the initial conditions – that is setting t=0 – one can derive Ω. This equation has a stable solution.

Note that a debt reduction policy will reduce a´ and thus shift the ISL curve to the left. This, however, would not hold if debt had exceeded a critical threshold: In such a case debt reduction could signal a lower future income tax rate τ^E and thereby stimulate consumption.

We now turn to the money market. Taking logarithms in equation (3a´) we obtain the following for the money market equilibrium

(3a") $m' - p = -\sigma_1 i - \sigma_2(i^* + a) + (z/ß)y + (1-z)a' - (z/ß)(v-u) - [(1-ß)z/ß] \ln L$

where m'= lnM and p = lnP; since $i = r + \pi^E$ (with π^E standing for expected inflation rate) we can draw the LML line in r-y space, or, alternatively in i-y-space. One should note that if one reads (3a") as a money demand equation which has to be estimated empirically we immediately see an identification problem with respect to the income elasticity of the demand for money which is z/ß; studies finding a unitary income elasticity implicitly argue that z=ß.

In r-lnY-space the LML curve will get progressively steeper the larger the ratio z/ß and the lower the interest semi-elasticity of the demand for money is. A debt reduction policy of government would shift the LML curve downwards. If the ISL curve remains in its initial position we will see a depreciation of the currency which will stimulate net exports of goods and services and thereby shift the ISL curve to the right and the ZZL curve downwards.

In the modified Mundell-Fleming model – without taking into account the very long-term effect of investment – we find the following multipliers for y, r, e (appendix 1):

	dγ'	dγ	db'	dJ[4)]	dZ*
dy	>0[1)]	>0	?	?	>0
dr	?	<0	>0[3)]	?	>0
de	<0[2)]	>0	<0	<0[5)]	>0[6)]

Note that a debt reduction policy (db'<0) will bring about a currency depreciation which is in contrast to the short-term portfolio analysis (see appendix 4). Raising the ratio of government R&D expenditures to GDP could raise output: dy/dγ' > 0. If the marginal product abroad is rising relative to domestic marginal product of capital we will get a long term depreciation (if $\sigma_1\psi_J$ is sufficiently large). The Euro real exchange rate will appreciate if government R&D support is raised, if public consumption relative to output is reduced, if public debt-GDP ratio is increased, if foreign marginal product of capital falls and if foreign patents reduce.

Fig. B10: The Portfolio-Augmented Mundell-Fleming Model

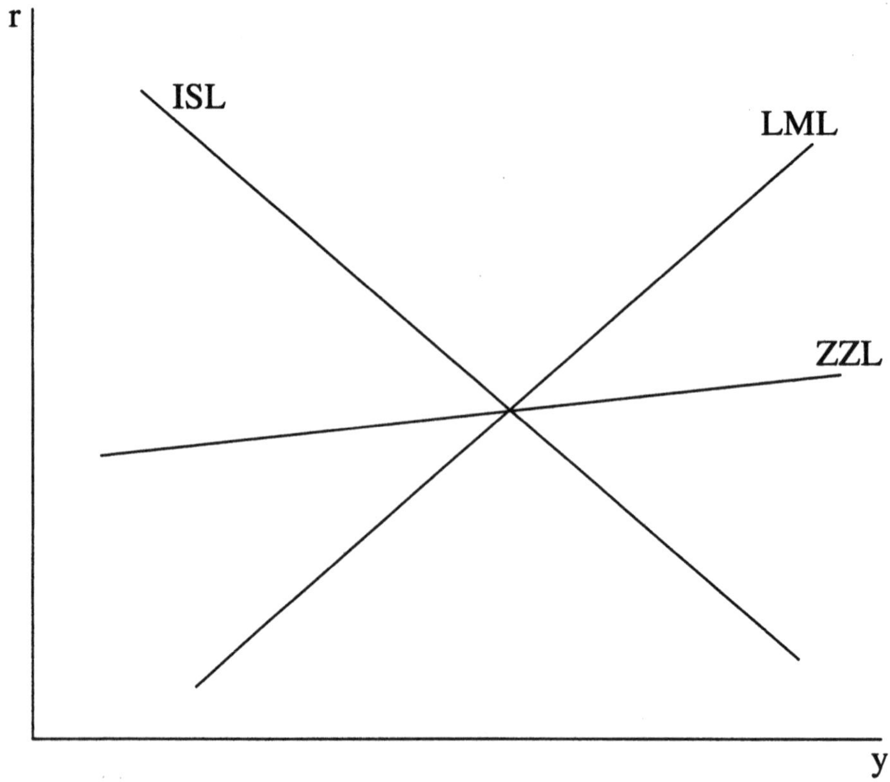

2.6. Supply-Side Fiscal Policy in a Schumpetrian Mundell-Fleming Model

We now turn to the standard Mundell-Fleming model in order to highlight the importance of supply-side aspects – within a Schumpetrian version of the model setup. In the traditional Mundell Fleming model expansionary fiscal policy is not really useful in a setting of flexible exchange rates. The traditional argument is that an increase in government expenditures will cause an appreciation which in turn will reduce net exports of goods and services, that is the initial rightward shift of the IS curve is followed by a leftward shift of the curve; and the balance of payments equilibrium line (ZZ) shifts upwards. This argument no longer holds if we distinguish between government consumption G and G′ which stands for growth-enhancing expenditures, e.g. R&D promotion. Raising G′ in the form of R&D promotion will bring about a higher rate of product innovation and process innovations, which will stimulate both net exports of goods and services. Moreover, as investment is stimulated – many product innovations can only be produced with new machinery and equipment on the one hand, on the other hand the marginal product of capital is raised by the accumulation of R&D capital – the IS curve will shift rightwards in the long term both because of higher sustained net exports and because of higher investment. There is, of course, some limit for government supply-side measures as government R&D support probably has rising marginal costs and marginally declining social benefits.

The modified Mundell-Fleming model reads as follows:

(8a) $Y = C(Y-T(Y), iB/P, i^*eF^*/P) + G + G' + I(r, Y_K(\ldots,Z(G'))) + X(q^*,Y^*,Z(G'))- q^*X^*(Y,q^*)$

where $q^*=eP^*/P$ and Z stands for the number of patents

(8b) $M/P = m(Y,i,A)$

(8c) $H(i,i^*,a, Y_K(\ldots(G')/Y_K{}^*) = X(q^*,Y^*,Z(G'))-q^*X^*(Y,q^*)$

where H stands for net capital exports

Equations (8a,b,c) represent the goods market equilibrium, the money market equilibrium and the balance of payments equilibrium

Fig. B11: Mundell-Fleming Model of Traditional Fiscal Policy under Flexible Rates

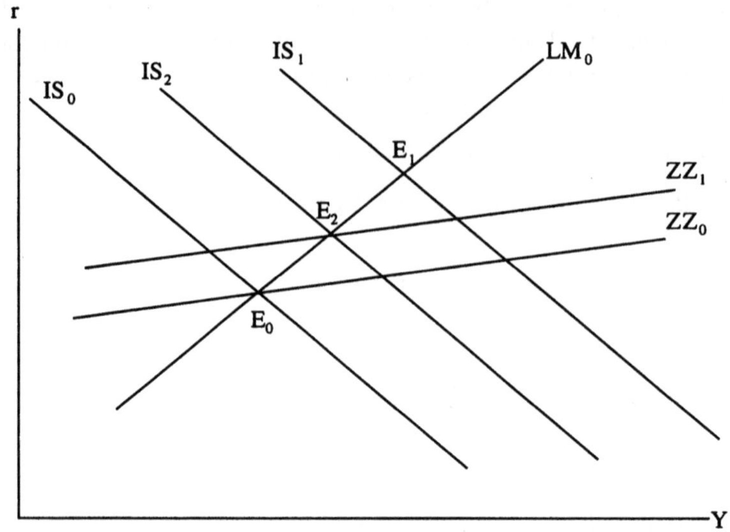

Fig. B12: Growth Enhancing Fiscal Policy in a Schumpeterian Mundell - Fleming Model

$\tan\gamma = dY^s/r = (I/\lambda)$

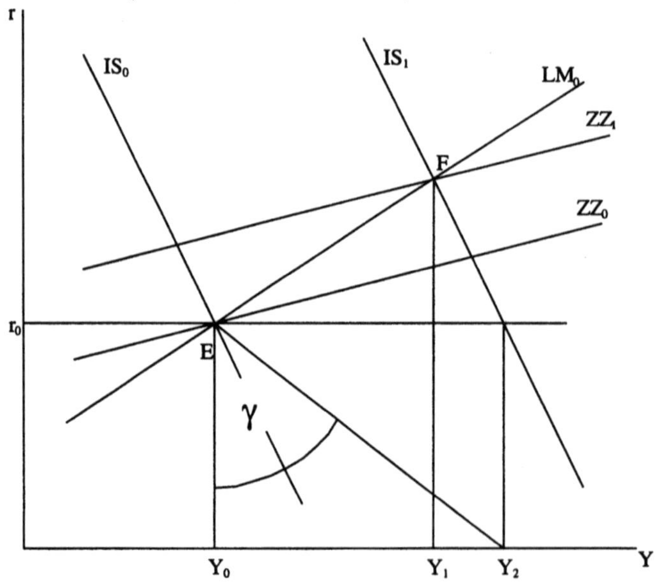

With R&D expenditures in Sweden – the OECD top performer in 1999/2000 – close to 4%, and facing a gradual increase of R&D-GDP ratios in OECD countries, one should carefully integrate R&D policies into the traditional Mundell-Fleming model.

2.7. Simple Interest Parity Model with Long Term Adjustment

As a final theoretical exercise we will focus on a one country model with a combination of short-term interest parity and long term purchasing power parity, the latter in the form of $P=\lambda eP^*$ where λ represents the terms of trade which depend on innovation (Z) and the efficiency and credibility of economic policy (D). One may assume that the real exchange rate is influenced by the political credibility of the domestic and the foreign political system – including the respective central bank. A relative fall of the credibility of the domestic system will lead to an increase of the real exchange rate (downward rotation of the PPP-line in panel b) in the figure below)

The simple model consists of the PPP equation (8a), the domestic money market equilibrium in the form of equation (8b) where A" is real wealth in the sense of the real value of stock; interest parity as given by (8c):

(8a) $P=\lambda eP^*$

(8b) $M = Pm(Y,i,A")$

(8c) $i=i^* + (e^E - e)/e$

where e^E is the expected exchange rate. With different credibility C′ and C′* of the domestic and foreign central bank (or, more generally, the political system), respectively, the interest rate parity will have to be modified in the sense that one has to include a risk premium which can be assumed to be proportionate (positive parameter Φ) to C′*/C′:

(8c′)) $i=i^* + \Phi \ln C'^*/C' + (e^E - e)/e$

This equation basically argues that the home country will have to offer a higher rate of return than abroad where one can earn $i^* +(e^E - e)/e$. Suffices to note here that in a model where the foreign central bank enjoys a higher credibility – and reputation – than the domestic central bank there will be structural net capital outflows from the home country. Thus, the foreign economy will enjoy higher growth as it can finance a investment-GDP ratio and more innovation projects. Mobile real capital systemic competition across borders should lead to C′*/C′ converging to unity in the long run. It is crucial to understand that as long as this is not the case – with the home country enjoying a credibility advantage (disadvantage) - the home country will have a current account deficit (surplus) reflecting net capital inflows (outflows). From this perspective it is clear that structural net capital flows will affect the terms of trade.

We define a long term equilibrium by

(8d) $e^E = e$ and hence $i=i^*$

in combination with (8a) and (8b) which results in with A'' specified by {...}:

(8a´) $e = P/(\lambda P^*) = M/[\lambda P^* m(Y,i,) \{[K P^S/P] \exp\delta_0\}]$

In panel a) the interest rate parity line IP_0 is shown, panel b) shows the PPP-line in accordance with (8a). Panel c) is a 45 degree line, panel d) portrays money market equilibrium under the assumption of exogenous real output and real financial wealth (stocks). Note that in panel b) $tg\alpha=\lambda$. The terms of trade will be influenced – among other things – by the relative rate of product innovation. If the home country offers more and superior product innovations it will be able to fetch higher prices in world markets since the price of any export product j can be assumed to be determined by marginal costs k'_i plus a Schumpeterian top-up element s_i.

In the case that we want to distinguish between tradables (T-goods) and nontradables (N-goods) we have to restate equation (8a) as:

(8a") $e = P^T /(\lambda P^{T*})$

Defining the price level at home and abroad – using the weights θ and $1-\theta$ for nontradables and tradables, respectively - by the following two equations

(9a) $P = [P^N \exp\theta] [P^T \exp (1-\theta)] = P^T (\varphi)\exp\theta$

(9b) $P^* = [P^{N*} \exp\theta^*] [P^{T*} \exp (1-\theta^*)] = P^{T*} (\varphi^*)\exp\theta^*$

we obtain, using φ as the relative price of nontradables in terms of tradables, the equation

(8"´) $e = [P\varphi \exp 1/\theta]/ \lambda [P^*\varphi^* \exp 1/\theta^*]$

This refinement could change the analysis somewhat as

$tg\alpha = \lambda (Z/Z^*,...) [\varphi^*\exp 1/\theta^*][\varphi \exp -1/\theta]P^*$

Innovation policies can affect Z/Z^* and therefore the terms of trade, moreover – assuming for simplicity that $\theta=\theta^*$ - the ratio φ^*/φ will affect the equilibrium solution. If relatively rapid technological progress abroad, such as the use of the internet, reduces the ratio φ^*/φ the PPP line will rotate upwards so that the home country suffers a depreciation. In the following simple analysis we will, however, assume that φ^*/φ is constant.

We will cover the case of an expansionary monetary policy, the case of debt reduction and the case of an increase of the marginal product of capital abroad.

The starting point is equilibrium E and E´ in panel a) and d), respectively, where inflation at home and abroad is assumed to be zero. An increase in M shifts the MMY-curve (in equation 8b) in panel d) downwards (MMY_1). Given the sticky output price level we have an immediate fall in the interest rate (point C´), the interest rate is r_1 (we assume no inflation). Assuming that market participants take the new long term exchange rate (e^E) consistent with PPP into account for formation of the long term exchange rate e^E we will see the IP-line shifted upwards (IP_1). The exchange rate is overshooting in the sense that point C with exchange rate e_1 is realized in the short term, while the long term exchange rate is $e_1´$. As the domestic price level gradually increases, the real money supply falls and the excess demand in the money market will drive up the interest rate (moving from C´to D´on MMY_1). With higher interest rates there will be higher net capital inflows so that the depreciation pressure is fading away (moving from C to D in panel a). Should the price level of stocks increase immediately after the rise of the money supply, the MM curve will shift to the right (MMY_2) because the excess demand in the money market requires higher interest rates. Point F shows that we will observe only a small depreciation, which in turn could stimulate exports and profits – plus higher foreign direct investment inflows – so that the stock price index could rise further. Note also that profits accruing from foreign MNC subsidiaries also have increased in terms of foreign currency – after the devaluation.

Fig. B13: Expansionary Monetary Policy, Public Debt Reduction and Foreign Productivity Shock in a Hybrid Exchange Rate Model

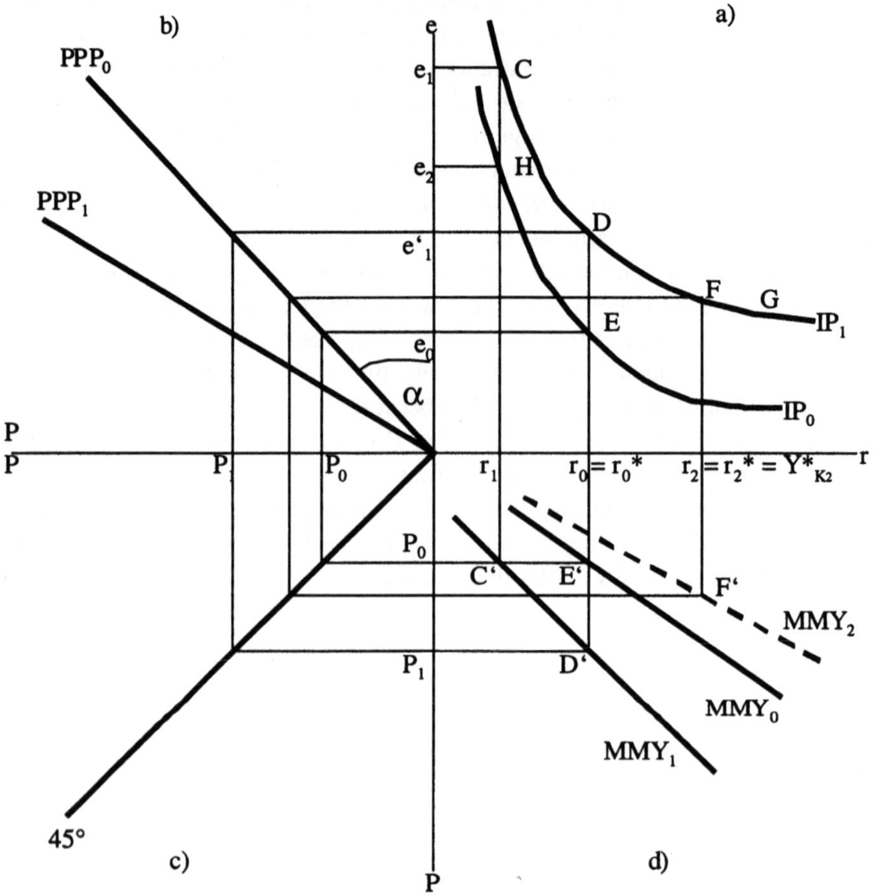

If government uses windfall tax receipts to buy back government bonds in the open market, net financial wealth A" will fall (we assume that there is no fully offsetting increase of corporate bond emissions and that the Ricardo-Barro equivalence theorem is not holding). The fall of A" will reduce the demand for money which implies a downward shift of MMY_0 (MMY_1). The IP curve is not shifting so that point H in a) is relevant. The case is similar to that of an expansionary monetary policy, that is there will be a strong initial depreciation followed by a modest appreciation, the overall result being a currency depreciation.

What happens if the marginal product abroad is increasing? We translate this case into a rise of wealth A" – that is domestic residents hold domestic and foreign stocks – which shifts the MMY2 curve downwards. If the PPP line is not shifting and we assume that the rise of Y_K* abroad translates into a rise of r* we have an upward shift of the IP line. It cannot be ruled out that long term equilibrium can only be reestablished if domestic output is falling: A reduction in Y will shift the MMY line downwards. Indeed output is likely to fall, since r is increased and investment I(r,...) will fall. With falling domestic investment Y is reduced. However, while GDP indeed is likely to fall GNP might remain stable or even increase, namely to the extent that domestic residents will raise the share of K* owned and thus receive higher dividend payments from abroad in the future.

Another potential interesting case is that of high (long-term) unemployment: if market participants anticipate that this would bring a more inflationary policy in the future – along with a less credible central bank – the IP-line will shift upwards and the PPP-line will rotate upwards. This also will cause currency depreciation.

Money Demand for GDP and Stock Market Transactions

We finally assume that money is not only used for financing transactions in goods markets but also for financing transactions in stock markets; the extended quantity equation is:

(B1) $M\, v(i, Y) = P\, Y + \alpha\, K\, P^K$

where α is the share of stock value traded per period. Using a Cobb-Douglas production function we get a long run equilibrium condition – assuming profit maximization

(B2) $M\, v(i, Y) = P\, Y + \alpha\, \beta\, P^K\, (Y/r)$

If one reads (B2) as a long term money demand equation one can write m^d(i, Y, q, r, A'') where A'' = K. Using Tobin's $P^K/P = q$ we obtain from (B2):

(B3) $M\, v(i, Y) = P\, Y\, (1 + \alpha\, \beta\, q/r)$

Assume that $\alpha\, \beta\, q/r$ is small we obtain after taking logarithms:

(B4) $\ln M + \ln v(i, Y) = \ln P + \ln Y + \alpha\, \beta\, q/r$; differentation yields

(B5) $d\ln M/dt + \varepsilon_{V,i}(dr + d\pi^E) + \varepsilon_{V,Y}\, d\ln Y/dt = d\ln P/dt + d\ln Y/dt - (\alpha\, \beta\, q/r^2)\, dr + (\alpha\, \beta/r)\, dq$

In a very simple setup, equilibrium holds where the MM curve – reflecting (B3) – intersects the investment equilibrium line II_0 which is vertical on q = 1 so that the price of existing real capital P^K is equal to that of new investment I. To the right of II_0 (above MM_0) there is an excess demand in the investment market (money market) which will raise investment and output. Equation (B5) shows that estimating – as done traditionally – M v(i, Y) = P Y gives biased results. As regards the extended quantity equation it is plausible to assume that the share of stocks actually traded positively depends on foreign direct investment inflows which – according to the Froot-Stein-Argument – depend on q* = eP*/P; moreover it will positively depend on the variability σ^{rs} of share prices (reflecting a rising stream of news).

Fig. B14: Long Term Equilibrium

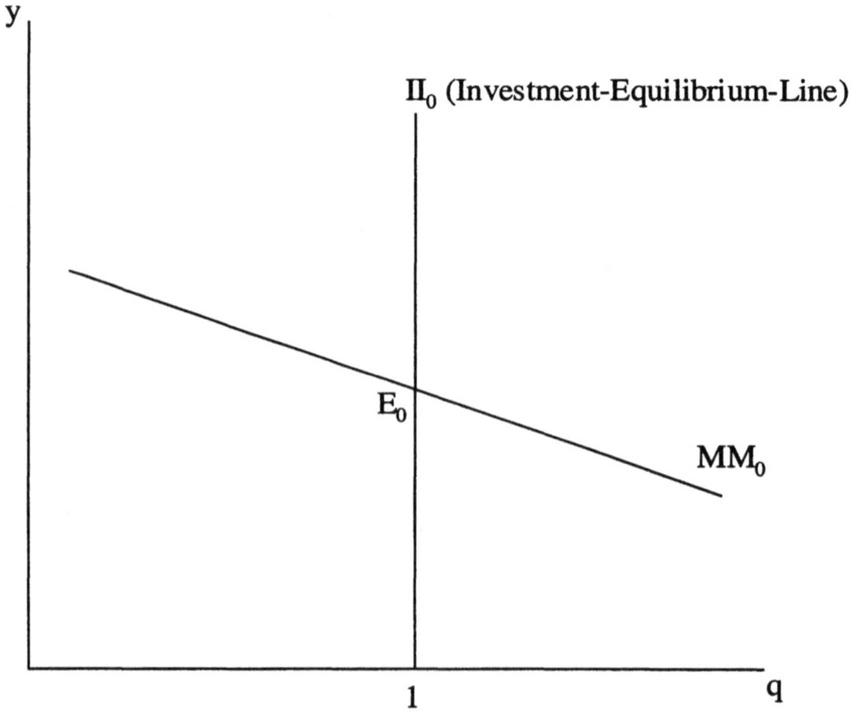

assumption is $|\varepsilon_{V,Y}| > 1$

3. Conclusions

We have shown that short and long-term exchange rate adjustments can strongly differ and that there are crucial implications for the theory of optimum currency areas. Debt reduction policies would be useful in the sense of bringing about an appreciation, however, only under certain circumstances (see appendix). The analysis has shown useful and innovative ways to combine portfolio analysis with the standard or an augmented Mundell Fleming model.

Debt reduction in Euroland countries without serious debt problems – such as Germany or France – is inadequate in the initial starting stage of a weak Euro. Market participants are unlikely to interpret debt reduction in such countries as a sign of improved government credibility – the case might be different for Italy – rather they will wonder why government is unable to identify growth-enhancing fiscal policies. To the extent that professionals do not head the ministries of finance in some Euroland countries the implication is that lack of competence translates into currency depreciation. Debt reduction in countries with excessive public debt might, however, be interpreted by market participants as a signal of higher government credibility which in turn will affect the terms of trade.

Further the conclusions to be drawn on the basis of the implicit two-country model are clear with respect to the goal of stabilizing the Euro:

- Governments of Euroland countries – especially Germany, France and Italy – should adopt a supply-side fiscal policy with emphasis on stimulating R&D and raising the net marginal product of capital; this also would stimulate capital inflows which could help to stabilize the Euro. It would be preferable to attract much higher FDI inflows into Euroland which are likely to emerge once growth prospects and rates of returns in Germany, Italy and France have improved. Germany's and Italy's dismal record of low FDI inflows – relative to gross capital formation – in the 1990s must be corrected.
- One can only warn against the proposal from the German ministry of finance which announced, in May 2000, that it wants to use large extra revenues from auctioning off UMTS mobile licenses and from privatization to pay back some 5% in government debt (with bad timing). There is no urgent need to suddenly reduce the absolute level of government debt given the fact that the debt-GDP ratio of Germany was slightly higher than 60% in late 1999. Buying back some DM 100 bill. will reduce future interest payments by about DM 6 bill. A preferable approach, however, is to raise growth by about 1 point equivalent to + DM 40 bill. which will translate into higher government revenues of DM 16-18 bill. UMTS license revenues are not necessarily a unique windfall event; rather the ministry of finance could generate some DM 50 bill. annually over several years if Deutsche Telekom AG were to be fully privatized – in itself a step to more growth in Euroland. Rather, adopting a broader tax reduction and

increasing government expenditures for R&D support (the R&D ratio fell in Germany from 2.9% in 1989 to 2.3% in 1999) and education plus special investment incentives for higher private expenditures on computers and internet equipment would be useful.

- A crucial topic for stabilizing the Euro is adopting economic policies in Euroland, which would switch transatlantic capital flows and affect long term exchange rate expectations favorably. US investors would invest more in Euroland if the return on investment were expected to rise in the Euro area. A reform of the public pension system in major EU countries, namely reducing the pay-as-you-go-system while introducing high tax incentives for investing in Euro stocks within private pension savings plans would be useful in two ways: the overall costs of labor will fall so that more employment will be created in Europe; moreover, the rising demand for stocks in Euroland will raise stock prices in the Euro zone – thus stimulating capital inflows into Euroland.

If governments in Euroland want to stabilize the Euro there also is urgent need:

- that ministers of finance really speak with one voice;
- that – facing windfall revenues – government debt reduction is not undertaken without careful analysis; in countries which clearly exceed the 60% debt-GDP ratio a debt reduction could be useful to the extent that markets will interpret this as a sign for a more rational government policy. In countries which are close to the 60% ceiling or below a superior alternative could be growth-enhancing fiscal policy programs and tax reductions, especially reductions in the corporate tax rate which would cause major increases in stock prices; corporate tax reductions are superior to simple income tax reductions if the aim is to achieve a major wealth increase in Euroland which is required to attract high capital inflows from the US and elsewhere. Distributions issues related to this strategy could be mitigated by adequate government policy.
- that Germany, France and Italy – the core countries with rather weak growth – undertake major structural reforms in labor markets and capital markets on the one hand, on the other hand adopt clear policies stimulating the expansion of fast broadband internet services offering large potential gains in factor productivity. The key to stabilizing the Euro is creating much improved growth prospects for the Euro zone.

The creation of the Euro has created new challenges for economics and for policymakers. An important policy challenge is to raise the marginal product of capital in Euroland by removing barriers to foreign investment and an equalization of marginal products of capital across borders. DE MENIL (1999) has pointed out several obstacles in this respect.

Finally one should note that the observation of a stock market boom (in country I) is not in contrast with the stock market parity equation. Rather incipient capital inflows will cause such a strong appreciation that we have overshooting – that is the second round impact governed by $g_e = g_{ps} - g_{ps^*}$.

In a comparative static perspective there will remain a modest appreciation, and the observer will witness a zigzag overall adjustment path. This, incidentally, is an argument for monetary policy not to strongly react to short term overshooting; unless such phenomena cause a critical epidemic-like revision of exchange rate expectations which tilt overall market sentiments towards strong (fundamental) reactions.

Economic globalization in the era of the new economy, rising skills of workers plus a higher R&D intensity of output are interesting phenomena which have not only real effects as adjustment costs and speeds are changing and opportunities for financial intermediation improving.

Important possible extensions of the models discussed concern above all an explicit two-country model, taking into account both tradables and nontradables and a more explicit modeling of stock markets. The reflections presented here are a modest step forward but they should also stimulate future research.

Appendix B1

Basic Long Term System of Three Equations (endogenous r, y, e)

(7.1”) $y - c(r, \tau, \tau^E) - j(r, \gamma', q^*, Y_K/Y_K^*) - \gamma - \gamma' + q^* x^*(q^*) = x'(q^*, \gamma') + y^*$; c_1, c_2,

$c_3 < 0$;

$j_1 < 0$; $j_2, j_3, j_4 > 0$

(3a”) $m' - p = -\sigma_1 i - \sigma_2(i^* + a) + (z/ß)y + (1-z)a' - (z/ß)v - [(1-ß)z/ß] \ln L$

(3c””) $x'(q^*, \gamma') + y^* + \psi(q^*, \gamma', Y_K/Y_K^*, \tau^E, Z^*) - p^* - x^{*\prime} = -\sigma_4 i/(i^* + a) + (1 + z/ß)y - (1-z)a' - (z/ß)v - [(1-ß)z/ß]\ln L - \ln F^*$; $\psi_1, \psi_2, \psi_3 > 0$; $\psi_4 < 0$; $\psi_5 > 0$

$m' = \ln M$

$a' = \ln A$; $A = M/P + B/P + eF^*/P$

$q^* = eP^*/P$; $\sigma_1, \sigma_2, \sigma_4 > 0$

$x' = \ln x < 0$; $x^{*\prime} = \ln x^* < 0$

Long Term Results[a]:

	dγ'	dγ	db'	dJ[4]	dZ*
dy	>0[1]	>0	?	?	>0
dr	?	<0	>0[3]	?	>0
de	<0[2]	>0	<0	<0[5]	>0[6]

[a] $DET = z/\beta\, [(c_r + j_r)(P^*/P\, (x'_{q*} + \psi_{q*}) + a'_3 F^*) + \sigma_4/(i^* + a)\, P^*/P\, (x^* + x^*_{q*} q^* - j_{q*} - x'_{q*})]$
$+ \sigma_1 [(P^*/P\, (x'_{q*} + \psi_{q*}) + a'_3 F^*)(1+z/\beta)\, P^*/P(x^* + x^*_{q*} - j_{q*} - x'_{q*})]$
$+ (1-z) F^* [-\sigma_4/(i^* + a) + (1+z/\beta)(c_r + j_r)]$
with $a'_3 = \partial a'/\partial(eF^*/P)$. Assuming $(x^* + x^*_{q*} q^* - j_{q*} - x'_{q*}) < 0$ we find $DET < 0$.
The long-term results refer to this assumption.

[1] $dy/d\gamma' > 0$ if $(1+j_{\gamma'} + x_{\gamma'})(P/P^*\, (x'_{q*} + \psi_{q*}) + a'_3 F^*) > (1-z)\, \sigma_4/(\sigma_1(i^*+a))\, (1+j_{\gamma'} + x_{\gamma'}) - (\psi_{\gamma'} + x'_{\gamma'})[((1-z)/\sigma_1)\, F^*(c_r + j_r) + P^*/P(x^* + x^*_{q*} - j_{q*} - x'_{q*})]$.

[2] $de/d\gamma' < 0$ if $|z/\beta\, [(c_r + j_r)(\psi_{\gamma'} + x'_{\gamma'}) - \sigma_4/(i^* + a)(1+j_{\gamma'} + x'_{\gamma'})] - \sigma_1 (1+z/\beta)(1+j_{\gamma'} + x'_{\gamma'})| < \sigma_1 (\psi_{\gamma'} + x'_{\gamma'})$; holds always if $\sigma_1 \to 0$

[3] $dr/db' > 0$ if $F^* \to \infty$, otherwise: $dr/db' = ?$

[4] Note that J is defined as Y_K/Y^*_K.

[5] $de/dJ < 0$ if $|z/\beta\, [(c_r + j_r)\psi_J - j_J\, \sigma_4/(i^* + a)] - \sigma_1 (1+z/\beta)\, j_J| < \sigma_1 \psi_J$.

[6] $de/dZ^* > 0$ if $|z/\beta\, (c_r + j_r)| > \sigma_1$.

Appendix B2

Modified Monetary Growth Model

It is useful to analyze the impact of a modified money demand function – with K/m as an additional argument in the function – in a monetary growth model. Denoting per capita output as *y and capital intensity as *k=K/L and real money stock per capita as *m we will use a Cobb-Douglas per capita production function f(...) with input factors capital K, labor L and real money balances m=M/P; here M is the nominal money stock and P is the price level.

(A1) y = f(*k,*m*) = V *kexpß *mexp(1-ß)

(A2) $d^*k/dt = sf(^*k) - (g_L + \delta)\ ^*k$,

where s is the savings rate, δ is the capital deprication rate, g_L is the growth rate of labor.

Real per capita money demand is, using a simple specification and restricting assets to real capital and money

(A3) $^*m = {}^*m^d(^*y, r, ^*k/^*m) = {}^*y\ (^*k/^*m)$ exp z e" exp-σi, where $0<z<1$

Under this specification in equilibrium we have

(A4) *m = *k exp (ß+z)/(1-z) e" exp-σi

The implication is that the per capita demand for real money balances is increased by the presence of the TOBIN-risk argument – here K/m – in the money demand function. While households hold money balances their could indeed be aggregate productivity spillovers for firms which benefit from the savings of transaction costs. This then is the reason why real money balances enter the production function (this then is a quasi-Romer output function).

Note that nominal interest rate i = marginal product of capital f_k plus inflation rate (g_P) so that per capita money demand can be written as

(A5) $(M^d/P)/L = {}^*m(f(^*k, ^*m), f_k + g_P - \delta^*, k^*/m)$

On the steady state growth path – with a constant real interest rate r – we therefore can write

(A6) $(M^d/P)/L = h(^*k, g_P)$

Growth of the real per capita money supply is given by

(A7) $d^*m/dt = (g_M - g_P - g_L)\ m$

where g_M is the growth rate of the nominal money stock M

As *m must be constant in equilibrium it must hold

(A8) $g_P = g_M - g_L$

Following the original TOBIN (1965) monetary model – who, however, used a conventional money demand function in his approach– we assume that households obtain money in form of a lump sum transfer v'':

(A9) $v'' = {}^*m\, g_M$

Disposable per capita income y" therefore is:

(A10) $y" = f(^*k,^*m) + v'' - {}^*m g_P = f(\,) + {}^*m(gM\text{-}gP) = f(..) + {}^*mgL$

Per capita output y equals per capita gross investment I/L plus per capita consumption C/L, where I/L consists of net investment d*k/dt plus (g_L +δ) which reflects the necessary investment for new workers and depreciation.

(A11) $f(^*k,^*m) = d^*k/dt + (g_L + \delta)\, ^*k + (1\text{-}s)\, y"$, where s=savings rate

In the steady state we have d*k/dt =0 so that we obtain as the steady state solution:

(A12) $sf(^*k, ^*m) = (g_L + \delta)\, ^*k + (1\text{-}s)\, ^*m\, g_L$

We find that per capita consumption C/L in the steady state is given by

(A13) $C/L = f(^*k,^*m) - (g_L + \delta)\, ^*k$

The optimum growth rate which maximizes per capita consumption is obtained from that steady state consumption which fullfills dc/dk=0. The golden rule still is the conventional PHELPS-rule:

(A14) $f_k = (g_L + \delta)\, ^*k$

The steady state capital intensity in this model setup can be higher than in the SOLOW model, while the original TOBIN monetary growth model suggested that a monetary economy would have a lower capital intensity than the nonmonetary SOLOW setup.

If both consumption and wealth entered the utility function of the representative individual so that U(C/L, k+(M/P)/L) the existence of money would raise the steady state utility level not only because a higher level of consumption can be reached but also because of the direct wealth effect; here per capital wealth is A/L = k +(M/P)/L.

An alternative way to modelling a positive link between money and growth is that one would assume that output uses „monetary intermediate products" in a modified version of the ROMER (1990) and GROSSSMAN/HELPMAN (1991) model.

If there are n intermediate bank products q^J which are combined to a final product $Y = [\Sigma(q^J) \exp\Omega] \exp 1/\Omega$ we will obtain – assuming identical cost structure across all intermediate products – the following final output Y (BRETSCHGER, 1998):

$$Y = q' \, n \exp 1//\Omega$$

where q' is the identical amount of each intermediate product.

We consider Y to be „investment products" Y^I. If one assumes that there is a constant price elasticity of demand for the differentiated intermediate product price can be calculated as a constant mark-up over marginal costs Q′. Profit maximization follows the Amoroso-Robinson condition:

$$Q' = p^q \,(1\text{-}1/|\varepsilon|) = p^q \,(1\text{-}(1\text{-}\Omega)) = \Omega \, p^q$$

It can be shown that $Y^I/Q = n \exp (1\text{-}\Omega)/\Omega$ where $0<\Omega<1$.

Hence productivity in producing investment goods is positively related to the number of intermediate products (here financial intermediaries). As n rises output will increase. This simple model, however, does not take into account trade and financial market integration, respectively, where benefits could stem both from a rising number of varieties and from economies of scale.

Appendix B3

Super-Long-Run Set Up (endogenous p, y, e)
(7a), (3a‘), (3c‘‘‘‘)
with condition β Y/K = r

Fig. B15: p-y-Model: Expansionary Monetary Policy

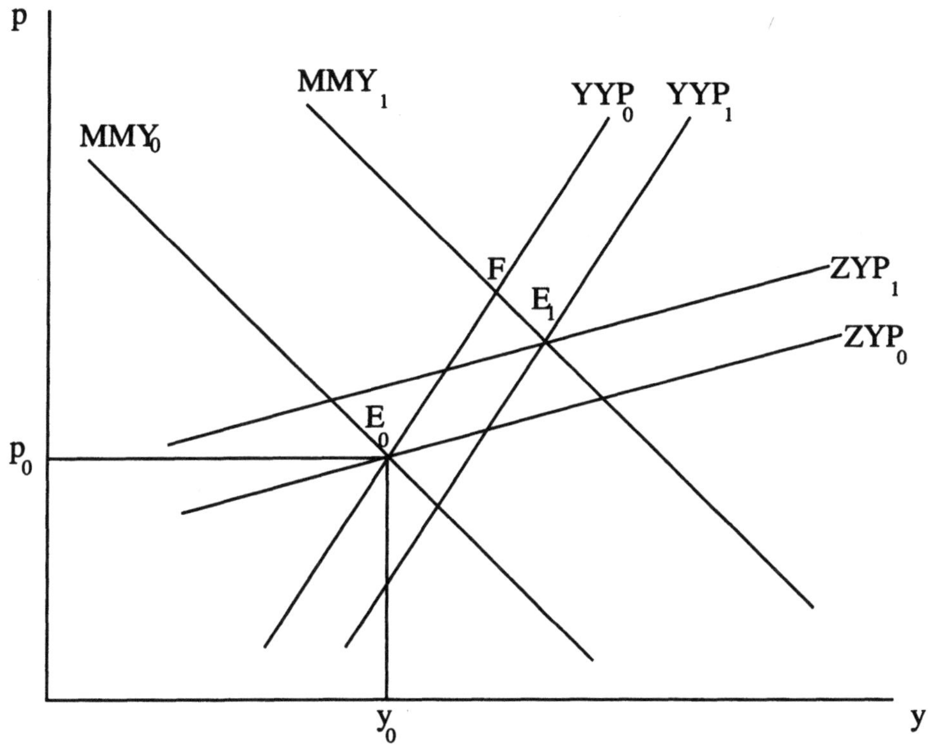

YYP: goods market equilibrium
MMY: money market equilibrium
ZYP: balance of payments equilibrium

Shift in YYP and ZYP due to devaluation.

Appendix B4

Short term results[1]: For the following system of equations

(3a') $M = Pm\,(r + \pi^e, i^*, a, Y, A, V(G'), L)$

(3c') $eF^* = Pf\,(r + \pi^e, i^*, a, Y, A, V(G'), L)$

	dG'	dB	dM
dr	>0[2]	>0	<0[4]
de	<0[3]	>0	>0

[1] $DET = (\, m_i\,(f_A - 1/(A_3F^*) - f_i\, m_A\,)\, A_3F^*$ with $A_3 = \partial A/\partial(eF^*/P)$.
Assuming $|f_i\, m_A| > |m_i\, f_A|$ we obtain DET > 0 (general assumption for all multipliers).

[2] Assuming $m_V = f_V$ and $|f_i| > |m_i|$.

[3] Assuming $F^* \rightarrow 0$ or $((m_V = f_V)$ and $(m_A > f_A))$.

[4] Assuming $f_A\, A_3\, F^* + m_A\, A_1 > 1$ with $A_1 = \partial A/\partial(M/P)$.

Appendix B5

Dependent Variable: DLOG(WKEURO)
Method: Least Squares
Date: 06/15/00 Time: 11:10
Sample(adjusted): 1994:03 2000:03
Included observations: 73 after adjusting endpoints

Variable	Coefficient	Std. Error	t-Statistic	Prob.
C	0.000802	0.001761	0.455630	0.6501
DLOG(WKEURO(-1))	0.115057	0.098011	1.173912	0.2445
D(DIL)	-0.013929	0.008701	-1.600760	0.1141
D(DIL(-1))	-0.022196	0.008450	-2.626841	0.0106
DLOG(QAKTIE)	0.275795	0.062973	4.379579	0.0000

R-squared	0.473712	Mean dependent var	0.002020
Adjusted R-squared	0.442753	.S.D. dependent var	0.019933
S.E. of regression	0.014880	Akaike info criterion	-5.511579
Sum squared resid	0.015056	Schwarz criterion	-5.354699
Log likelihood	206.1726	F-statistic	15.30168
Durbin-Watson stat	1.735280	Prob(F-statistic)	0.000000

$$dlne_t = a_0 + a_1\, dlne_{t-1} + a_2\, d(i_t^{long} - i*_t^{long}) + a_3\, d(i_{t-1}^{long} - i*_{t-1}^{long}) + a_4\, dlnP^S/P^S_t{}^* + \varepsilon_t$$

Fig. B16: Euro Exchange Rate Based on Estimation 1994.03 - 1999.03; forecast 1999.04-2000.03

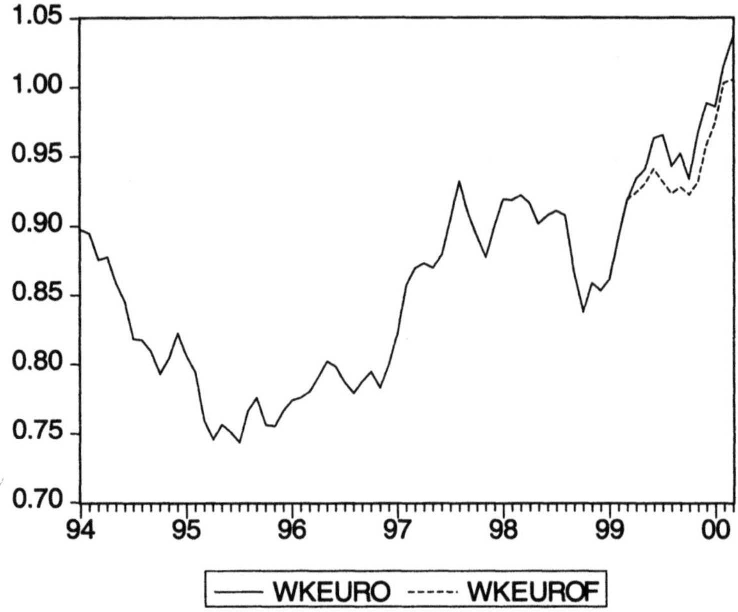

C. Exchange Rate Policy for the Euro: Theory, Strategic Issues and Policy Options

1. Introduction

With the start of the Euro and the European Central Bank (ECB) there is a new monetary regime within the EU. In a global perspective the introduction of the Euro means that the number of major currencies is falling sharply; the global monetary system looks more oligopolistic than before, but it also looks more symmetrical in the sense that the US and Euroland are economic heavyweights of similar magnitude. In principle the switch to a reduced number of currencies could mean economic benefits not only because transaction costs are saved but also because global crisis management might become easier with a smaller number of actors and more equal heavyweights (Tab. A6). At the same time currency competition will intensify which should stimulate financial innovations possibly undermining financial market regulations and stability, respectively.

While in late 1998 many anticipated a depreciation of the dollar at the start of the Euro the actual developments were characterized by a weakening Euro. A main reason for this was the positive transatlantic growth and interest rate differential in the first half of 1999 when Italy and Germany had poor growth rates of less than half the US figure of 3-4%. The high growth rates of Ireland, Spain, Portugal, Luxembourg and the Netherlands – above or close to 3% in 1999 – are an insufficient counterweight to the modest growth in the core of Euroland, namely Germany-Italy-France, where France is doing somewhat better than Germany. The three big countries have not only high unemployment rates and low growth rates, but they also face the problem of rather low employment ratios where Italy had a very low figure of about 70% in 1998/99, whereas France and Germany were slightly higher with 73 and 75%, respectively. Compared to Norway, Denmark and the US this is almost 10 percentage points lower – too low, as a matter of fact. Lack of political reforms and structural change in the core of Europe undermined the new Euro which does not yet have the reputation the DM used to have. There is little doubt that the Kosovo War raised the uncertainty about EU developments further, and this undermined the Euro which fell between January 4 and June 1 from $ 1.18 to 1.04. The main influence on the Euro falling under parity to the dollar in early 2000 was, however, relatively high US economic growth (and higher US interest rates) and the fact that purchasing power parity suggested a rate of around 0.9 – at least if we follow the arguments of the Austrian WIFO institute.

A temporary devaluation might pose a minor problem, but a strong and ongoing devaluation vis-à-vis the dollar and the yen could make the Euro look like a loser in the first critical year. From such a position it will be difficult to become a respected international currency. Moreover, a continuing devaluation would undermine the political support for the Euro in several EU countries because many citizens in Euroland are likely to (mistakenly) take the depreciation of the currency as a signal that the Euro will be more inflation prone than the DM or the Dutch Guilder or the Austrian Shilling used to be.

Since the creation of Euroland means that so much more trade than before is internal, the incentive for government and the ECB to avoid a strong Euro depreciation might indeed not be very strong. However, one must warn against a strategy which considers a weak Euro in its infancy stage as a benign neglect problem. What could be a tolerable strategy is inadequate in the beginning of a currency union. Markets have reacted strongly to the political pitfall of EU finance ministers accepting that Italy – facing weak growth – could have a 2.4 deficit-GDP ratio instead of the promised 2.0 figure. In the critical early stage of reputation-building markets consider the critical countries with high debt-GDP ratios in Euroland (Italy, Belgium) as particularly important; if they show signs of poor political will to fulfill the stability and growth pact this could point future political tensions; once that bell weather is over asymmetric shocks or a general economic downswing could show that Euro countries are unable to fulfill the agreed convergence criteria and the long-term goal of the stability and growth pact: very low budget deficit-GDP ratios. It is obvious that the dollar and the British pound benefit from the Euro weakness as international investors substitute Euro for the greenback or the pound. Euroland lacks – as is also emphasized subsequently – a consistent growth strategy. At the same time in the wake of the reinforcement of price transparency in the EU, Euroland might face a stronger tendency of labor-intensive industries to relocate labor to nearby eastern Europe. This could cause critical long-term unemployment in some industries which, however, also reflects lack of structural change and low labor mobility in Euroland. We will have to ask how the world can live with a weak or strong Euro and how international monetary relations will change under the impact of Euroland. As will also be shown one must raise the issue of a pro-growth policy in Euroland.

The topic of EMU and international economic relations has been discussed by relatively few authors (MUNDELL, 1993; JOHNSON, 1994; EUROPEAN COMMISSION, 1997a; McCAULEY, 1997; MASSON et al., 1997; KENEN, 1998) where issues raised mainly concern the potentially declining share of the US dollar in the international monetary system, the question of a depreciation versus appreciation of the Euro, some problems of transatlantic monetary cooperation and the functioning of the G-7 and G-10 groups after the start of the Euro. In the following analysis we will take a different approach and focus on transition problems in the first stage of the Euro on the one hand, and on the other hand we will focus on long-term problems including issues of foreign direct investment and global crisis management. While flexible exchange rates generally facilitate the control of the money supply and thus are helpful in achieving ECB credibility, one may doubt that the traditional US policy stance would be adequate for Europe. The US largely pursued a benign neglect attitude according to which market forces should determine the exchange rate, even if this included large deviations from purchasing power parity (PPP); an exception was the Plaza Accord which sought to moderate a strong dollar appreciation trend which undoubtedly was prone to fuel protectionist forces in the US. A strong overvaluation of a currency – misalignment "from above" – is an implicit subsidy to imports of goods and services and an implicit subsidy to foreign direct investment outflows and net capital exports, respectively; with a given overvaluation there is, of course, no equivalence to a domestic interest rate reduction since the currency overvaluation concerns only tradables – not the nontradables sector – and since the mirror effect is an undervaluation of the currency of major partner countries whose export sector will be stimulated artificially.

An important issue will be whether the ECB will adopt a benign neglect attitude towards exchange rate movements which, if followed by a similar US attitude, could lead to very large exchange rate fluctuations. While the world economy has learned to live with considerable temporary exchange rate volatility without major problems, one may argue that long-term misalignment is a major policy problem. A special problem could occur in the transition to a new international portfolio equilibrium and a higher share of EU (Euro) currencies in global currency reserves. A gradual build-up of Euros in global foreign exchange reserves requires sustained current account deficits of Euroland which, however, is likely to start with a high surplus – to the tune of about Euro 100-150 bill. in the late 1990s. Only a strong Euro appreciation or a very high EU growth rate could bring about the required swing in the current account position of Euroland. A relatively high growth rate of Euroland would be easier to accept for the US than a strong Euro appreciation; the equivalent dollar depreciation could be prevented by high US interest rates which, however, would undermine global economic growth.

With high capital mobility there is a general need for more exchange rate flexibility worldwide, requiring partly flexible exchange rates vis-à-vis the dollar; however, in a regional context of countries with strong trade links and similar per-capita-incomes, fixed parities with wide margins (EMS I worked better with +/- 15% than with very tight earlier margins) are needed. While flexible exchange rates have the general advantage of facilitating the central bank's control of the money supply, excessive exchange rate movements – both overshooting and long-term misalignment – can undermine the efficiency of investment decisions and resource allocation, respectively. Moreover, it can cause serious national and international stabilization problems as well as negative welfare effects which could emerge as a consequence of rising nominal interest rates and currency substitution.

To the extent that the Euro will become a major international reserve currency in the long term, there is a rising international responsibility of the ECB and the EU, respectively. At the same time there is an enormous internal responsibility of the ECB which will be eager to pursue its goal of price stability –

starting with a favorable 1.5% inflation record in early 1999 – and thus could be inclined to avoid temporary depreciations of the Euro although divergent business cycles in Europe and the US could warrant such a development. The Maastricht Treaty requires that the ECB support economic policy goals to the extent that price stability is not undermined, and the favorable starting inflation record allows the ECB to indeed conduct a slightly expansive monetary policy. There is, however, some risk that conflicts between the ECB and the ECOFIN over budget consolidation and the Stability and Growth Pact, respectively, render a consistent policy mix quite difficult. Since the weak initial reputation of the ECB and the three year starting period 1999-2002 imply a relatively weak Euro in the beginning, whereas the incentives for private investors to restructure portfolios in favor of the Euro along with the prospects of the UK – with the financial center of London – joining Euroland after 2002 imply a long-term appreciation, one should not be worried about temporary Euro depreciations provided they are modest. Since the Euro´s role as an international reserve currency will be reinforced in the long run, a gradual appreciation of the Euro is likely.

The Euro will compete against the US-dollar and the yen which, however, is a weak competitor both because of the continuing Asian financial crisis and because of the tacit Japanese banking crisis which is part of an overall economic stagnation scenario. In a long-term perspective the Asian crisis which forces Japan to open up its formerly sheltered financial system could be exactly the required catalyst for a long-term revival of an otherwise rather weak currency.

For the EU the start of the Euro means facing strategic decisions with respect to the exchange rate policy both within Europe and vis-à-vis the US. It is well-known that politicians in some countries – most notably in France – consider the launch of the Euro as an opportunity to start a new Bretton Woods system of fixed exchange rates in which Euroland would be on equal terms with the formerly dominant US. However, there are also arguments in favor of a flexible exchange rate system which could bring more or less external exchange rate volatility than in the ECU period.

In the following analysis we will focus on some issues of optimum currency areas and derive some principles for a rational exchange rate policy. A Euro exchange rate policy will affect the global international monetary system and thus have both internal European and external effects. Since exchange rate policy traditionally is the domain of policymakers – and not so much of central bankers – one has to discuss the role of fiscal and monetary policy coordination in Europe. There is, of course, also a need to focus on the G-7 activities since it was the G-7 group which established the Louvre and Plaza Accords which emphasized medium-term consensus about exchange rate policies in a transatlantic and transpacific context.

The degree of exchange rate flexibility clearly is important for the control of the Euro money supply process. Flexible exchange rates facilitate controlling the money supply. If the ECB is to acquire a high reputation internationally, it will have to not only achieve low long-term inflation rates but also to achieve such a record in a way which makes its monetary policy approach credible. Certainly one will have to distinguish transitory problems of ECB´s monetary policy efficiency which are related to initial uncertainty about model parameters in the new Euroland setting from the more crucial long-term topic of pursuing a consistent monetary policy in an effective way.

An important issue will be whether or not the ECB should pursue dirty floating; in particular there could be the delicate question whether or not the ECB should encourage temporary depreciations of the Euro in order to stimulate the Community´s exports so that higher export growth would help to reduce high unemployment rates in core EU countries.

In Section 2 we will focus on fundamental issues of exchange rate policies including aspects of high capital mobility and overshooting plus the topic of incentives for a weak Euro policy which could aim at improving the unemployment situation in Euroland via a gradual nominal and real Euro depreciation; considering potential alternatives in the form of tariff protectionism and similar options, we find that a beggar-thy-neighbor policy could be attractive for Euroland under certain conditions. In section 3 the focus is on the European Monetary System Mark II. The final section offers some conclusions. The bottom line of the arguments presented is that the introduction of the Euro could increase global exchange rate stability.

2. Exchange Rate Regimes and Exchange Rate Policies

As regards the assignment of competencies to the ECB and the ECOFIN the Maastricht Treaty gives a strong mandate in exchange rate policies to the ECOFIN which will make decisions about formal international exchange rate agreements. However, the clause which requires unanimous decisions of the ECOFIN gives the ECB a relatively strong position in exchange rate policy (Fig. 1). If the ECB and the ESCB, respectively, can establish a successful stability-oriented monetary policy – a difficult challenge if fiscal policy and wage policies would impair high economic growth in Euroland – a rising ECB reputation could help to limit the ECOFIN's power. Major conflicts undermining the ECB's reputation are likely in the context of the problem of excessive (national) foreign exchange reserves and of excessive gold reserves. Governments could decide to run down excessive reserves rather quickly while stability of the international monetary system could require gradually reducing excess reserves.

Fig. C1: ECB and ECOFIN Policy Assignment

ECB [General] Issues recommendations to ECOFIN on exchange rate systems and on parity adjustment	ECOFIN [General] Decides unanimously on agreements of the formal exchange rate system (after recommendation of ECB and Commission); Parity adjustment decisions made via qualified majority voting (ECB/ECOM recommendation); General orientation for exchange rate policy in the absence of formal exchange rate systems; Possible ECB goal of price stability should not be impaired.
ECB [ERM] Has the right to initiate deliberations on parity changes; Can suspend interventions; Will be requested to agree on parities with ECOFIN and national central banks of non-Euro countries	ECOFIN [ERM] Ministers of Euro countries and other EC countries agree on parities with ECB within ERM II; Ministers not in ERM II or Euro area have no vote.

With the Euro a new international monetary system is emerging. Such a system is characterized by four distinct features:

- the exchange rate regime
- the principles of international crisis management
- the choice of preferred foreign exchange reserves
- the mechanisms for eliminating external disequilibria

The exchange rate regime will be a mixture of fixed exchange rates with the EMS-II and of flexible exchange rates vis-à-vis the US dollar. New principles of international crisis management have yet to be agreed upon; the lack of new rules became apparent when Mr. de Silguy of DG II complained of not being fully informed about IMF plans for coping with the Asian economic crisis in 1998. It also is unclear whether Euroland will be represented as a single entity in large international organizations – possibly with the combined voting power of national member states – or if Euroland is to be represented by all Euro countries which then would be expected to vote unanimously on matters of common interest. The choice of preferred foreign exchange reserves largely is an informal one guided by economic rationality; above all it concerns the structure of official foreign reserves of central banks outside Euroland on the one hand, and, on the other hand, the structure of reserves held by the ECB and the national central banks of Euro countries.

Finally, there is the topic of how to cope with external disequilibria. Euroland can be expected to record a modest current account surplus in the starting period, but this might change in the long run. To the extent that the Euro is becoming a major international reserve currency Euroland could afford modest long-term current account deficits. What would happen in the case of large surplus or deficit positions of Euroland? Taking into account the fact that – at least based on figures for Germany (DEUTSCHE BUNDESBANK, 1998) – the import and export elasticities for trade with countries outside the EU are much smaller than for intra-EU trade, necessary corrections could be achieved only by relatively large exchange rate changes; for example, one would have to accept large shifts in the Euro-dollar exchange rate. Judging by German figures the sum of domestic and foreign import elasticities would be much below unity after 1999 so that the Marshall-Lerner condition is violated, which in turn implies that the exchange rate is not very useful for correcting trade account imbalances. This then implies that imbalances would have to be corrected mainly by adequate transatlantic growth differentials; i.e. a deficit position of Euroland would have to be corrected by contractionary fiscal and monetary policy which would bring about the required reduction in output growth and import demand in Euroland. This, of course, raises problems of how to achieve an adequate policy mix in a setting in which the ECB has to cooperate with Euro-XI finance ministers.

As regards reserve requirements of the ECB and Euroland, respectively, it is clear that there is a potential excess supply of US-dollars and gold (Tab. A3/A4) to be expected since the creation of the Euro implies that roughly half of EU international trade is becoming internal trade in Euroland (assuming here a full long-term overlap of the EU and Euroland). It is conceivable to allocate excessive US dollar reserves of EU countries in a way which makes it the basis of a new capital-funded social security system in Europe. An alternative would be a voucher type assignment of such funds to private households which then could decide either to spend them on consumption or on savings.

Is a considerable medium-term current account deficit of Euroland likely? As regards the growth of exports of goods and services relative to import growth one may expect that high growth rates of post-socialist eastern European economies will reinforce a modest growth of net exports in the long run so that the trade surplus of Euroland could increase. Instead of trying to predict the trade balance position by focusing on growth rates of exports and imports of goods, one could focus on the evolution of capital imports so that the trade balance position is rather perceived as reflecting the development in the capital account position.

As the capitalization of bond markets and stock markets of Euro-11 countries reached only about half the size of the US figure (66% and 44% of GDP at end-1997 in comparison to 117% and 129% in the US; see Tab. A1) in 1997, an optimistic perspective on Euroland is that the integration of EU financial markets and the dynamic efficiency gains to be expected from the introduction of the Euro will lead to higher market capitalization in both bond and stock markets of Euroland. In late 1999 the volume of the Euro bond market indeed had increased strongly.

Expansion of bond markets will partly reflect volume growth in the sense that relatively more firms will rely on the stock market and on corporate bonds as a means to finance investment in Euroland in the future – with a figure of $149 bill., corporate bonds outstanding in Euroland played a tiny role relative to the US with a figure of $3025 bill. in late 1997; however, there should also be a role for major capital gains (and a reduced role of bank credits in the EU in the long run). This suggests high Euroland capital inflows in the medium term, so that net capital imports would be reflected in a negative current account balance. Parallel to this development one may anticipate that the dollar share of international debt securities issues would fall from more than 50% in 1997 to a somewhat lower figure, while the Euro share would rise correspondingly (EU currencies accounted for 1/3 of new issues and of the stock of international debt securities issues in 1997; see appendix). Rising capital inflows of Euroland would, of course, stimulate an appreciation of the Euro vis-á-vis the dollar.

As regards the use of major currencies on one side of foreign exchange transactions, EMS currencies, including the ECU, accounted for 70% of the 200% global total, with the DM representing about 1/2 of the EMS figure; the DM, the pound sterling and the French franc accounted for 37%, 10% and 8%, respectively in 1995 (IMF, 1997, p. 171); the Swiss franc represented 7%. Even with a sound ECB monetary policy and sustained economic growth in Euroland, it will take many years to challenge the dominant US dollar which is dominant as an international finance and reserve currency. With European cross-currency trading eliminated in Euroland the dollar could gain transitorily after 1999 and 2002, respectively, but it is doubtful that the US dollar can maintain its dominant position easily in the long run. Euroland´s influence in the international currency competition will be reinforced once the UK joins Euroland since London – jointly with New York – is the world´s leading financial center. With the UK joining Euroland the Euro area will become more dependent on the US business cycle. In the very long run this interdependency could be weakened by an eastern EU enlargement in combination with an eastern enlargement of the Euro area.

The Euro exchange rate regime and the exchange rate policy will focus on four broad areas (Fig. 2): first, the exchange rate vis-à-vis the US-dollar; second, the Euro exchange rate policy concerning the type of link established between the

Euro and the EU outsiders; third, the link between Euroland and the east European accession countries; and finally, the link between the Euro and other currencies; implicitly the latter question also concerns the link between the Euro and African countries which adopt the Euro in the context of continued special monetary relations with France (CFA zone) and Portugal, respectively. The crucial topic is not fixed versus flexible exchange rates but rather how much exchange rate flexibility is optimal for the four groups. Since exchange rate policy has to take into account the n-1 country problem one cannot, of course, adopt consistent Euro exchange rate policies without developing a common view on policy principles within a transatlantic context. The G-7 meetings, talks at the BIS as well as bilateral cooperation between the ECB and the FED will be important in this respect.

Fig. C2: Areas of Euro Exchange Rate Policy

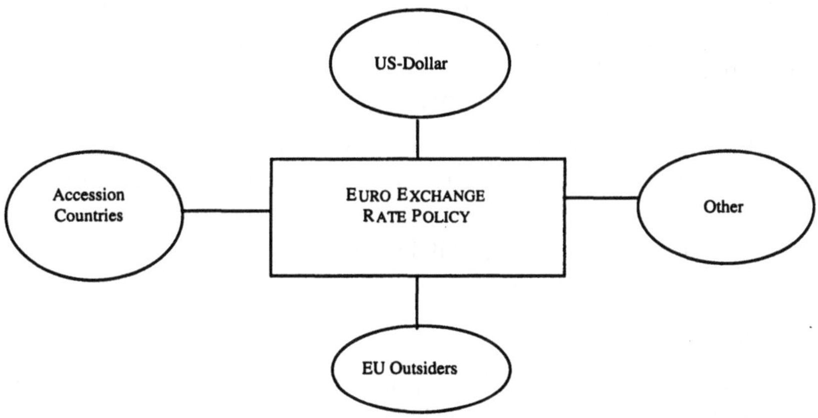

2.1. Exchange Rate Regimes in the Era of High Capital Mobility and High Technology Competition

Since the switch to flexible exchange rates in 1973 there has been enormous nominal and real exchange rate volatility. For example, the DM was at 1.71 to the dollar in early 1980 – a first bottom value of the DM which had experienced a rather gradual nominal appreciation over the previous years. However, by 1985 the dollar had rallied strongly and reached 3.47 in February 1985. In mid-1986 the dollar had fallen under DM 2; in April 1995 it fell to an all-time low of 1.36. In 1997 it hovered around 1.80. Will we see similar exchange rate changes of the Euro vis-à-vis the dollar or even stronger exchange rate variability?

Theoretical Aspects

With a continuing increase of international capital mobility and the thereby growing divergence between adjustment speeds in slow goods and factor markets and very fast financial markets, one may anticipate major overshooting effects (DORNBUSCH, 1976) and magnification effects (BILSON, 1979). Nominal exchange rate movements therefore could have considerable real effects, especially if deviations from purchasing power parity (PPP) are long-lasting. Potentially, these problems will be aggravated by the integration of capital markets in Euroland raising adjustment speeds in financial markets.

According to empirical analysis deviations from PPP played a major role in the 1970s and 1980s. To date the reasons for this are rather unclear. One could argue, however, that the impact of a more intensified global innovation race have not been taken into account in theoretical and empirical analysis. Since the international innovation race intensified strongly after 1974 one should see an increasing technological specialization of R&D and of output and exports, respectively. Indeed, in the 1980s the US and Japan pursued a stronger R&D specialization, but Germany and the EU – for various reasons – did not (WELFENS/ AUDRETSCH/ADDISON/GRUPP, 1998).

If the US specializes very successfully so that it can generate additional first mover advantages in world markets while the EU is relatively weak in product innovations and specialization, one should expect a real appreciation of the dollar. The real Euro exchange rate q will fall which is consistent with the following modified PPP equation for tradables:

(1) $P^T = qe\, P^{T}*$ (* for US)

where P^T and P^T* are composed of a price index P^s for standard tradable products and a price index P^i for innovative technology-intensive products

(2) $P^T = (P^s)\exp ß(P^i)\exp(1\text{-}ß),\ 0<ß<1$
(3) $P^T* = (P^s*)\exp ß*(P^i*)\exp(1\text{-}ß*),\ 0<ß*<1$

For the US equation (2) holds mutatis mutandis – with starred variables. A spurt in US product innovations implies that P^i* will rise relative to P^s* and to P^i (expressed in US-dollars); if process innovations would dominate over product innovations in the US one might, however, witness a relative fall of P^i* since more process innovations imply falling product costs and thus falling relative prices; rising US profits could, however, stimulate US FDI inflows.

There is a need to focus more extensively on the role of these two types of innovations in real exchange rate determination.

The real Euro exchange rate could increase in the long run as EU firms catch up with the US in terms of innovativeness. In the era of economic globalization which is a period of intensified international technological competition – with periods of spurts in innovation and of changing technological leadership – there is a need for higher real exchange rate flexibility. This implies for the concept of fundamental equilibrium exchange rates (WILLIAMSON/MILLER, 1987) that a wider nominal band – a broad target range – should be envisaged, especially in a post-1999 environment.

In addition to the innovation related reflections about long-run exchange rate movements one has to also consider the fall in transaction costs in international financial markets which implies for a given increase in the international interest differential higher capital flows – mainly short-term capital flows – than traditionally. This itself will amplify real exchange rate volatility.

It is clear that the analysis has to be conducted here in terms of monopolistic competition and foreign direct investment. While an innovation boost in the US – in particular in the field of product innovations or in sectors with dynamic economies of scale – should bring a temporary real appreciation of the US-dollar, one should not expect a permanent increase since product cycle trade and transatlantic foreign direct investment will support a successful catching-up process of Western Europe.

2.2. Trade, Foreign Investment and Exchange Rate Adjustment

In the era of economic globalization in which foreign direct investment flows are growing fast relative to trade, the problem of functional exchange rate regimes and policies cannot be discussed without taking into account some links between FDI, trade and exchange rate movements. This holds not least because changes in the real exchange rate will affect FDI flows, whereby a Euro depreciation will raise FDI inflows into Euroland (FROOT/STEIN, 1990). High exchange rate volatility generally can be expected to reduce the investment output ratio and investment growth (empirical evidence: WELFENS/JUNGMITTAG, 1997), respectively, since volatility is part of investment risk in the tradables sector; this risk aspect also applies to the nontradables sector to the extent that FDI is not restricted in this sector.

Since about 1/3 of OECD trade is intra-company trade, i.e. trade within multinational companies, it is clear that exchange rate policies which distort FDI indirectly will affect trade relations.

Theory of Optimum Currency Areas

Euroland is not an optimum currency area since labor mobility across countries is low and since the specialization of output and exports might further increase in the future. However, the reduction of transaction costs in Euroland implies trade creation effects within Euroland so that the degree of openness will increase – the

McKinnon criterion therefore is satisfied by Euroland. The Vaubel-criterion according to which countries facing high structural adjustment pressure should have high real and nominal exchange rate flexibility is not really an argument against EMU with the 11 country starter group; increased relative price changes across sectors (and countries with their respective sectoral specialization) could indeed bring about required real exchange rate shifts. A more important aspect according to a more recent theory of optimum currency areas (TAVLAS, 1993) concerns the net gain in credibility of monetary policy in Western Europe – here not so much the Euro per se but rather the creation of the ECB is a favorable aspect. The Euro should also bring global efficiency gains since there is now a viable alternative to the dollar when – in a long-term perspective – it comes to the question of choosing a vehicle currency. Intensified international competition between the US-dollar and European currencies – i.e. the Euro, the pound and the Swiss franc – could help to reinforce the stability orientation of all major central banks worldwide. Finally, one may emphasize that the Euro and the ECB, respectively, will facilitate global crisis management.

Fig. C3: Optimum Currency Area Issues

Labor Mobility (Mundell)
Openness (McKinnon)
Diversification of Output/Exports (Kenen)
Structural Adjustment Pressure (Vaubel)
Credibility (Tavlas)
External Savings of Transaction Costs [Vehicle Currency]
Global Crisis Management

The principles of exchange rate policy concern several fields: (1) the choice of monetary strategy; (2) the exchange rate volatility issue; (3) the problems of international crisis management; and (4) the issue of dealing with temporary PPP deviations. It is still unclear whether certain devations from PPP are not effectively reflecting transatlantic shifts in global innovation leadership. In the late 1990s Germany (and Sweden) improved the global patent share in five of the ten fastest growing technology fields while the US improved its position only in three fields (Japan in two fields) – while being a clear global leader in the internet. Euroland might indeed improve its innovation record and thereby raise growth and the real interest rate which in turn would stabilize the Euro.

Fig. C4: Principles of European Exchange Rate Policy

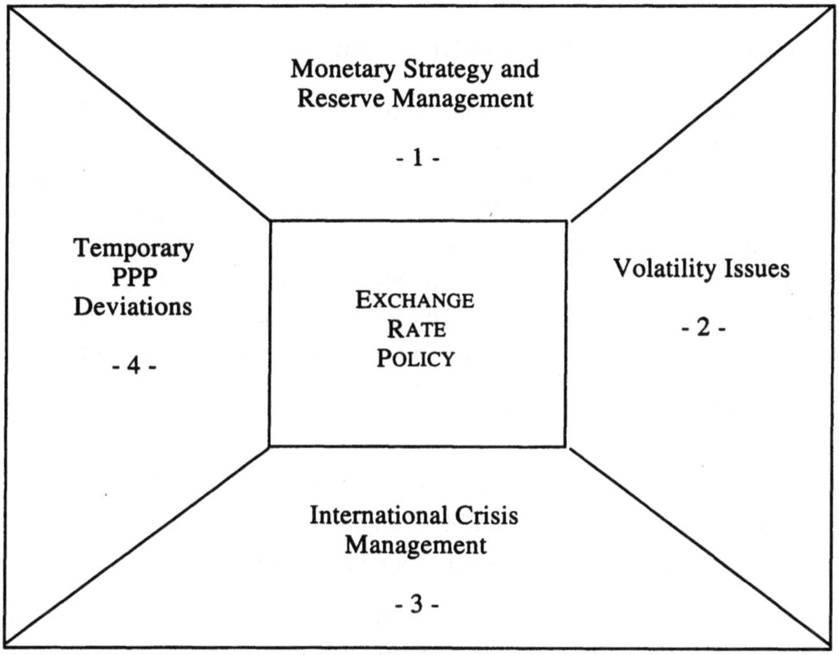

In an era of increasing capital mobility there is the question to which extent one should tolerate temporary deviations from purchasing power parity. It would be important to make public statements on this issue because current and expected exchange rates influence the purchase of goods and investment decisions. With reduced uncertainty there should be more efficient investment decisions. Limiting long-run exchange rate uncertainty is indeed important for both domestic and foreign investment. Somewhat linked to this issue is the volatility issue which in turn is linked to expectations and changes in money supply strategies in the US and Euroland. There are some arguments which suggest that short-term exchange rate volatility will increase but also arguments that let one expect that exchange rate volatility could reduce temporarily.

A potentially crucial issue is global crisis management. The Asian crisis has shown the extent to which regional shocks can translate into large regional exchange rate adjustments and that overshooting phenomena are relevant. Given the size of international short-term capital flows one might consider concerted US-EU action at some point, but instead of putting too much emphasis on joint intervention – possibly in conjunction with the IMF – it would be wise to emphasize mechanisms to avoid Asia-type crises. Improved information and monitoring of global short-term financial flows could be crucial in this respect as well as a strengthening of the BIS.

2.3. Some Aspects of the Euro-Dollar Exchange Rate

Since OECD countries have learned to live with rather volatile dollar exchange rates, even high Euro-dollar volatility should not pose major problems in principle. However, exchange rate volatility negatively affects investment (WELFENS/JUNGMITTAG, 1997) so that a rational exchange rate policy will try to dampen "excessive" volatility. An important question is whether switching from ERM to EMU will increase the variability of the dollar exchange rate. Dynamic simulations (BENASSY-QUERE/MOJON, 1998) suggest a negative answer.

Major impulses for exchange rate movements should be the following:

- differences in monetary growth rates or changes in the ratio of $m'^{Euro}/m'\$$, ($m'=\ln M$);
- differences in output growth in Euroland and the US;
- the transatlantic interest rate differential; and
- other impacts (including speculative bubble effects).

Both the monetarist (M) model of the exchange rate and the Dornbusch (D) model suggest this although the reaction of the exchange rate to changing transatlantic interest rate differentials has different signs in these two models. A relative increase of the Euro interest rate will cause an appreciation of the Euro while the monetarist model suggests a depreciation. The main reason for these different reactions is that with sticky prices (Dornbusch model, equation 4) the liquidity effect will dominate in the short run; a rise of the interest rate indicates a restrictive monetary policy. Under flexible prices (M model) rising interest rates indicate an expansionary, inflationary monetary policy, so that the Fisher effect is crucial. A somewhat different exchange rate behavior is suggested by models with currency substitution. If one assumes that the nominal interest rate reflects expectations of the growth rate of the nominal money supply we have an additional term – compared to the monetarist model (equation 5) – which suggests that the domestic currency will depreciate if the variance of nominal interest rates Var(i - i*) increases (see equation 6). A strong impact of this term can only be assumed with relatively strong risk aversion (e.g. GÄRTNER, 1997).

(4) $e_t = m_t - m^*_t - (y_t - y^*_t) - \mu^{-1}(i_t - i^*_t)$ [D model]

Note: assuming open interest rate parity, the interest differential can be replaced by the expected devaluation rate E(a) or, taking into account the formation of expectations, by expected money supply differentials E(m)-E(m*).

(5) $e_t = m_t - m^*_t - (y_t - y^*_t) - ð(i_t - i^*_t)$ [M model]

(6) $e_t = m_t - m^*_t - (y_t - y^*_t) - (a + ð)(i_t - i^*_t) + bVar(i_t - i^*_t)$ [CS model]

To the extent that the creation of the Euro in fact reinforces the integration of financial markets in a transatlantic context, the role of risk aversion should indeed reduce because the variance term itself should reduce in the long term. Interest rate volatility in Europe should also reduce because the Euro means a closer integration of capital markets across EU countries.

Fig. C5: Topics of Exchange Rate Policy

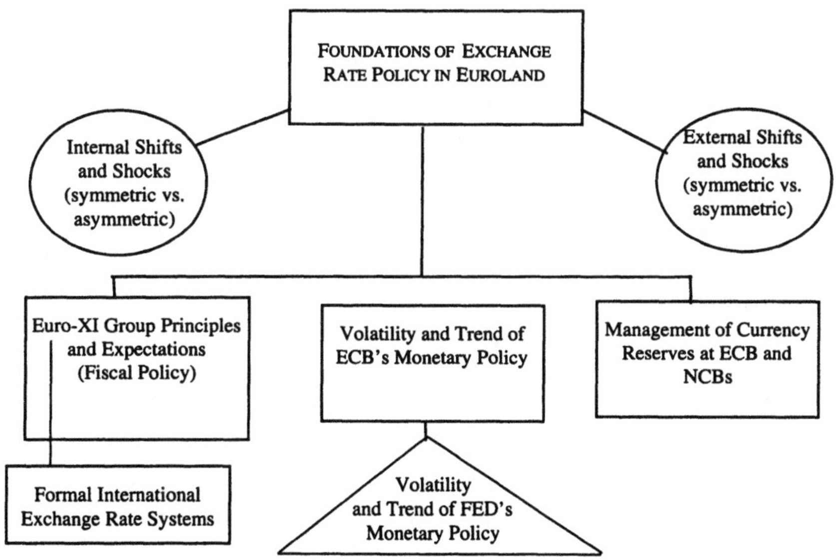

In the case of asymmetric shocks it will be important whether the subgroup of countries concerned in the Euro area will develop consistent fiscal policies at the national level and whether wage policies at the national and regional levels are flexible enough to accomodate shocks without a strong rise in unemployment. Asymmetric shocks are a long-term challenge which differs from the initially rather imperfect synchronization of business cycles across countries – in the long term synchronization should increase. Long-term economic growth in Euroland can be fostered by a credible, stability-oriented and transparent monetary policy of the ECB provided that its volatility is rather low; this requires that national central banks in Euroland not run down their respective national foreign exchange reserves. A consistent ECB monetary policy would help little with respect to long-term exchange rate stability and predictability, respectively, if the US Fed would not adopt a similar policy strategy. From this perspective it will be crucial to develop a continuous transatlantic policy dialogue, where the US probably will have strong incentives to include Japan in this process. In periods of major misalignments an effective policy dialogue within the G-7/8 framework is indispensable; however, the traditional policy stance of leaving exchange rate determination fully to market forces might render the correction of strong misalignments a difficult task. As the Asian crisis in 1996/97 has shown a strong, temporary devaluation of the yen, combined with a dollar appreciation – and East Asian NICs' currencies fixed to the dollar – was sufficient to trigger a severe international economic crisis which could have been avoided if one had chosen both parities with wide margins (and options for timely devaluation to correct for strong real appreciations via a relative rise of the price level in NICs) and a more market-determined banking system in NICs – including a comprehensive reporting system which would indicate the ratio of short-term to long-term capital flows. One can, however, not overlook the strange Japanese monetary policy which had brought about very low nominal interest rates inviting foreign speculators to take Yen demoninated loans which carried –-under an open position – high risks with respect to potential Yen appreciation. From the perspective of global responsibility abnormally low nominal interest rates in Japan are dangerous and unacceptable.

The foundations of exchange rate policy in Euroland will be related to monetary policy (volatility and trend) and to the management of currency reserves at the ECB and the national central banks (NCBs). It also will be related to the Euro-XI group with its informal coordination of fiscal policies.

Two crucial questions remain. First, will differing transmission processes in Euroland and the US cause a rising role of divergent monetary policy paths in Euroland and the US; different balance sheet structures of major Euro countries (BORCHERT, 1998) imply that it will be difficult to predict the effects of ECB monetary policy and that the transmission process itself will change over time in Euroland. Intensified competition in financial markets in Euroland will bring about some cross-country harmonization of banks' balance structures. The second point concerns temporary differences in output growth of Euroland and the US. The Euro itself reinforces intra-EU trade links and thus weakens transatlantic interdependency in business cycles. This effect could be reinforced by shadow effects of an eastern EU enlargement. This could reduce exchange rate variability.

Finally one has to consider the role of interest rate differentials, which basically can be decomposed into real interest rate differentials and liquidity plus inflation plus reputation differentials. Since the Euro facilitates foreign direct investment in a transatlantic context one may anticipate a narrowing of the real yields on investment in Euroland and the US. The present high divergence between e.g. US and German marginal products of capital – with the German (and French) value reaching only ¾ of the US figure – will not be sustained. This suggests some real and nominal interest rate convergence. A successful, stability-oriented ECB will accumulate a reputation over time and therefore will narrow the reputation gap vis-à-vis the US FED in the long run. This would imply a reduced interest rate differential. Whether the ECB really will be successful in the reputation game is an open question.

2.4. Global Crisis Management

An aggressive exchange rate policy with a focus on deliberate devaluations is dangerous for international economic stability since such a strategy not only is an inadequate beggar-thy-neighbor policy but also impairs the climate for international policy cooperation in periods of international economic crisis. Such a crisis can start with crucial policy failures in a single nation or a major region of the world economy. From this perspective it is particularly important for Euroland and the US to reach a new consensus about principles of a sound exchange rate policy. Such principles could include the rule that sustained high current account imbalances should lead to a depreciation of the respective currency in a gradual manner, and that any major regional crisis in the world economy will be considered as a problem to be solved in common interest.

The lesson of the Great Depression has been that national policy failure – a very restrictive US monetary policy in 1929-33 – can translate into a global economic crisis if international government cooperation and/or international monetary cooperation is inadequate. While the creation of the BIS and the IMF reinforced postwar monetary cooperation via international organizations there is still the challenge of international government cooperation and of international monetary cooperation in a period of crisis. From a triade perspective it is crucial that cooperation in both policy fields is achieved and that the two fields themselves are coordinated so as to achieve an adequate – if not optimal – policy mix. As long as US political and economic leadership goes along with adequate US action and parallel actions of major international organizations dominated by the US one might expect an implicit international coordination within the triade in periods of international economic crisis. However, the economic weight of the US is declining in the world economy in the long term (TILLY/WELFENS, 1997), and the political power of the US in international organizations also is weakening (e.g. judged by the evolution of the Shapley value).

Fig. C6: International Policy Organization

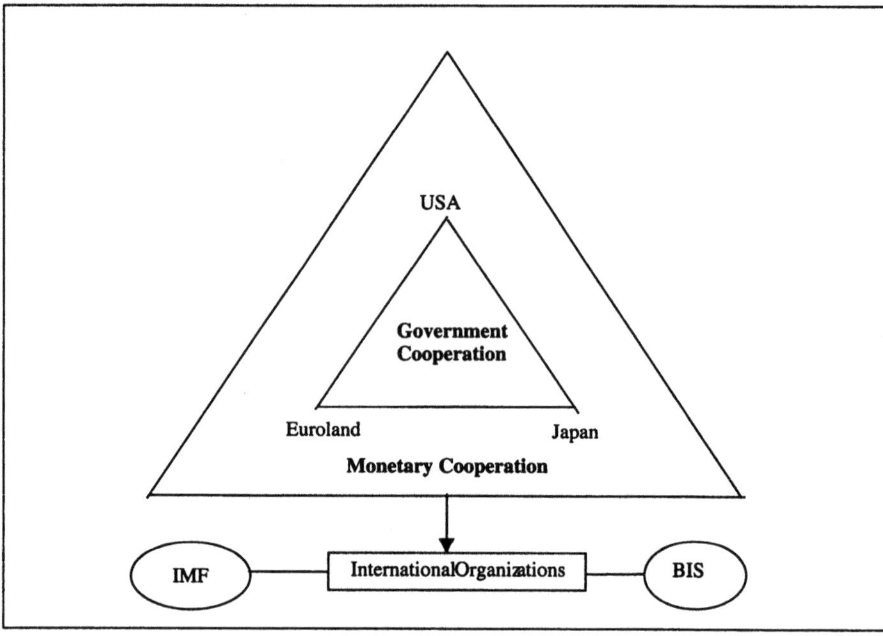

The Euro starts in the period of a major Asian crisis in which Japan´s economic weakness, including problems in the financial system, are confronting the US and Euroland with negative external effects. Informal coordination at G-7/G-8 meetings where fiscal policy coordination should be on the agenda was not achieved prior to 1999; informal monetary cooperation was also rather weak within the BIS framework. Thus there is reason to assume that the policy mix within the triade is not optimal, and one may doubt that deliberations on the Stability and Growth Pact even considered the issue that Euroland might have to play an active fiscal and monetary policy role in a period of a global economic crisis. The political independence of the FED and the ECB, respectively – established for good reasons (with emphasis on price stability in the EU) – is valuable in normal times, but it is unclear whether in a period of a looming global economic crisis there will be serious attempts in Europe, the US and Japan to achieve a proper policy mix and consistent international coordination in both fiscal and monetary policy at the same time. One option for remedying this problem is to change the statutes of the Bank of International Settlements and to reinforce its role in monitoring monetary policy worldwide in normal times and in particular to create a secretariat concerned with global monetary policy coordination in periods of an international economic crisis. If the Euro should achieve a similar international role as the dollar, the US would raise the issue of burden sharing in a new way – expecting the EU to assume a greater responsibility and to contribute more in co-financing multilateral financial rescue packages.

2.5. Looming Protectionism of Euroland?

Within Euroland some countries – notably France and Italy – seem to favor a Euro depreciation strategy as a means to solve domestic unemployment problems. With the creation of Euroland the EU will increasingly perceive itself as a specific identity and therefore could indeed consider options to exploit its leverage as a large economy in the world market. Following the standard literature on optimum tariffs it is obvious that a large country could improve its terms of trade via imposing an import tariff, the optimum being the inverse of the import supply elasticity E according to traditional trade theory. However, the traditional optimum tariff theory does not consider the role of foreign direct investment. Taking into account the role of outward foreign direct investment (WELFENS, 1998b) one finds for large countries which are major source countries of foreign direct investment that the optimum tariff rate is smaller than suggested by traditional approaches. The optimum import tariff is $(1/E)(1-h)x^*$, where x^* stands for the export-GDP ratio of the exporting country (country II) and h is the share of capital owned by multinational companies (from importing country I) in the exporting country´s export sector. The basic reason behind the modified optimum tariff rule is that import tariffs imposed by a country which is a major source country of foreign direct investment tend to reduce the profits accruing to subsidiaries abroad whose production partly goes to the markets in the country where the parent company is located. Since Euroland is a major source country of FDI and a considerable share of its imports actually is from subsidiaries abroad which are owned by EU firms, one may anticipate limited tariff protectionism on the part of Euroland.

The protectionist issues could become more important, however, in a transatlantic economic setting if conflicts in the field of exchange rate policy or of monetary policy coordination should emerge in a way which leads either the US or the EU to resort to import restrictions as a bargaining chip in order to achieve concessions in other policy areas.

Having lost many protectionist options due to the WTO rules and EU monitoring of subsidies the option of a Euro depreciation – including talking down the Euro or weakening it by uncooperative behavior of some ministers of finance – could be politically attractive if Euroland were unable to restore full employment.

3. The EMS Mark II

The creation of the Euro should lead to more integrated financial markets which reinforce the efficiency of factor allocation both because exchange rate volatility plays less a role as a disturbing factor after 1999/2002 and since the efficiency of financial markets is strengthened. It is, however, unclear whether the creation of the Euro will increase correlations across all financial market segments in Euroland, while there are some arguments that transatlantic synchronization could be weakened at least in calmer periods giving more monetary policy autonomy to the ECB than was enjoyed previously by the Deutsche Bundesbank. The Deutsche Bundesbank (1998, p. 67/68) writes:

"Whether these correlations will increase further for the participating countries with the start of EMU is fairly doubtful, especially in the case of the share market. For one thing, exchange rate uncertainty is already low at present, and, for another thing, the degree of synchronization in the share markets currently appears to be somewhat exaggerated by the continuing worldwide stock market boom as it usually increases during phases of rapidly changing prices....If financial market turbulence occurs more rarely in the Euro area owing to the elimination of exchange rate-related crisis and asynchronous monetary policy courses, the correlations between the national markets could even decrease on a longer-term average, so that they would more strongly reflect the remaining enterprise-specific and sector-specific return and risk factors. Concerning the correlations in the short-term price or interest rate movements against non-EMU countries, one particularly interesting consideration is whether the German capital market, once it has been subsumed into a Euro-wide financial market, will be more dependent of price or interest rate movements in the United States. One indicator which suggests that this could be the case is that a larger and more liquid market has a greater resistance to foreign influences. That must not necessarily be so, however....A close price synchronization is likely to continue to result primarily from symmetrical investor expectations in the two markets....In calmer periods the latitude for decoupling depends on how sharply the price-determining fundamental factors of the respective countries diverge."

3.1. Transition Problems of Euro-Latecomers

Denmark and Greece will be members of the EMS II which creates currency satellites fixed to the Euro-core. The UK and Sweden will probably have to join EMS II at some point if they are to fulfill the modified post-1999 convergence criteria (here: exchange rate stability). Adherence to ERM II is voluntary. With margins of +/- 15% there is a wide band which should allow the accommodation of asymmetric shocks without giving up the parity itself. Intervention to stabilize an outsider currency can be stopped by the ECB if such interventions endanger price stability in Euroland. The overall convergence process in the EU-15 group achieved low inflation rates in all countries by 1998 so that there is no reason to anticipate strong fundamental devaluation needs vis-à-vis the Euro in the Euro starter period 1999-2002. At the same time Euro outsiders have an incentive to shadow Euroland's monetary policy and to maintain or seek full EMS membership since this will bring nominal and real interest rates that are almost as low as in Euroland itself. The fact that UK interest rates were clearly higher than DM interest rates in 1996/97 points to potential interest disadvantages of Euro outsiders.

From a strategic point of view there is no reason not to allow parity changes of Euro outsiders in the transition period provided that this brings benefits for both sides: the ins and the outs. However, parity changes probably would be small, especially since devaluations could be taken by market participants as a signal of further future devaluations which in turn would warrant a risk premium in the bond market.

A serious problem could emerge if the UK were to abstain for a prolonged period from Euro membership. Since the UK business cycle is more dependent on the US cycle than Euroland, there could be cyclical reasons for pound-Euro exchange rate changes. If speculative attacks on the Euro should emerge a strong appreciation of the pound is likely. British industry and foreign investors in the UK will face disadvantages under such circumstances. If the ESCB were forced to raise interest rates strongly EU unemployment (ADDISON/WELFENS, 1998) could rise.

3.2. Transition Problems of Accession Countries and Exchange Rate Regimes

An important aspect of exchange rate policy concerns the role of east European accession candidates. It is clear that accession countries will have to accept the *acquis communautaire*, including independence of the central bank and convergence reports. Introducing the Euro is not required by EU membership automatically. Most east European accession countries are eager to join the Euro as soon as possible so that – once they are an EU member country – they would not have to remain in the EMS II for an extended period. One can only warn against such a strategy. The main reason for not fixing the nominal exchange rate of a relatively poor country is the fact that in the course of economic catching-up the relative price (P^N/P^T) of nontradables to tradables will rise; from a theoretical perspective a shift in the price ratio of nontradables to tradables in country I relative to country II could change the nominal exchange rate in a system of flexible rates. The positive correlation between this relative price movement and per capita development was observed by KRAVIS/LIPSEY (1983, 1987); ASEA/MENDOZA (1994) showed that economic opening-up and growth bring relatively high productivity growth to the tradables sector which could explain the relative price increase of nontradables. At the same time one may notice that price differentiation for tradables still plays a role in a wider Europe as RICHARDS/TERSMAN (1996) observed that food prices in Latvia reached only about one-third of the Swedish price level in 1994.

The Choice of the Exchange Rate Regime in Transforming Economies

The global economic monetary system is shaped by the triade and the global organizations active in this field, mainly the IMF and the Bank of International Settlements (BIS). Transforming economies of eastern Europe have achieved in a first stage current account convertibility – usually referring to foreign residents – which is the basis for trade and growth-enhancing international economic relations. IMF membership is a natural part of achieving current account convertibility, but later capital account convertibility also has to be considered. While for transforming economies official capital inflows are the typical starting point for integration with the world capital markets the long term capital account liberalization should help to foster two-way capital flows, including foreign direct investment inflows which are crucial for covering net imports of goods and services (foreign exchange perspective) and for modernizing the supply side of the economy. The choice of the exchange rate regime is a crucial decision to be taken by the political system in transforming and developing countries. The following analysis is mainly concerned with transforming postsocialist countries of eastern Europe but the general theoretical arguments extend well beyond this country group. In the following analysis we summarize some key arguments form the literature but also advance some new ideas on the choice of the exchange rate regime. A basic proposition will be that fixed exchange rates are the more appropriate the stronger institutional arrangements support stability-oriented monetary policy and free trade policy.

From an economic perspective the nominal exchange rate and the rate of change over time are important for various reasons, where focus here will be on a devaluation (the case of an appreciation is symmetric):

- The nominal exchange rate times the world market price tells producers which goods are worthwhile to export: Whenever marginal costs are smaller than the domestic equivalent of the world market price there is an incentive to export. A nominal depreciation raises export revenues in domestic currency terms and therefore stimulates exports (and a depreciation makes imports more expensive so that imports will be reduced). This statement is only true if – with given world market prices, say in US dollar, – the domestic price level has not increased by a higher percentage than the nominal exchange rate: Indeed, export quantities and import quantities are determined by the relative price ratio eP^*/P.

- The nominal exchange rate determines relative cost advantage in the sense that the international wage ratio eW*/W (with W* representing the wage rate abroad and W the wage rate in country I) is crucial for any investor considering alternative locations for investment. If e is rising so that we have a devaluation in a fixed exchang rate regime or a depreciation in a fixed exchange rate regime foreign wage rates become relatively higher than the initial ratio indicated so that the export sector is expending. The import competing sector also can grow. The relative wage perspective is related to the above argument and basically reinforces the role of the (real) exchange rate as a means for adjusting the balance of payments.
- If there is a macroeconomic disequilibrium in the sense of a large and unsustainable current account deficit a devaluation – or a depreciation over a certain period in a setting of flexible exchange rates- can bring about the necessary correction: Exports will increase and imports reduce, more strictly: the value of exports will be raised while that of imports will fall so that the initial excess demand in the foreign exchange rate market will be eliminated over time. In a system of flexible exchange rates there is immediate adjustment so that there is no sustaining excess demand or supply in the forex market.
- The exchange rate also will have an influence on foreign direct investment. A rise of the exchange rate makes acquiring industrial assets cheaper for foreign investors so that the overall investment-GDP ratio could incrase. However, one cannot rule out that domestic investors will reduce investment in a fully offsetting way – assume that these firms have foreign debt, then after the devaluation or depreciation the domestic value of debt has increased.
- The exchange rate indeed is relevant for calculating the domestic currency equivalent of government and private foreign debt. A depreciation by x percent will raise the internal equivalent of the foreign debt. Note that for investors willing to invest abroad the economic significance of the devaluation rate is different: The effective rate of return abroad is the sum of the foreign interest rate i* plus the devaluation rate (de/dt)/e over the relevant holding period. In contrast to the uncovered interest rate parity condition $i = i^* + (de/dt)/e$ the covered interest rate parity requires that i is equal to the foreign interest rate i* plus the swap rate (f′-e)/e where f′ stands here for the forward exchange rate.
- The exchange rate will have an influence on the price level since many goods incorparate intermediate imported inputs whose prices go up with the exchange rate. Moreover, profit-maximizing firms in import-competing industries will raise prices as import prices go up after a devaluation or currency depreciation; and firms in the tradables sector will raise domestic prices after devaluation or currency depreciations since the alternative of selling abroad is possible at higher prices. While a rise of tradable prices might be considered to be an inflationary impulse it not necessarily is equal to inflation; if other prices –

namely the price index for nontradables – are reduced the aggregate price index still could be constant.

The exchange rate regime is directly relevant for monetary policy and hence ability to control the inflation rate. In a system of flexible exchange rates the central bank has full control over the money supply so that political responsibility for undesired inflation rates is easy to assign. In a system of fixed exchange rates the central bank can control only the domestic credit element of the overall money supply, but every intervention in the foreign exchange market will have monetary effects via a change in the stock of foreign reserves. If there is an excess demand for foreign exchange the central bank must sell an adequate amount of its reserves which means that the money supply is reduced; conversely, if there is an excess supply of foreign exchange at the going parity (assume for the moment that there is no corridor around parity) the central bank has to buy foreign exchange which implies that the stock of the money supply is incrasing.

This brings us to the strategic five aspects of the exchange rate regime; the simplified issue of fixed versus flexible exchange rates concerns:

- The central bank´s ability to control the money supply process.
- The ability of the political system to cope with balance of payments problems and with foreign debt problems.
- The option of policymakers to fight domestic disequilibrium – unemployment – with measures beyond pure monetary and fiscal policy.
- The integration of national goods and financial markets with international markets – assuming that the higher the exchange rate volatility (could be high in a fixed exchange rate regime as well as in a regime of flexible rates) the less intense is the international integration of markets. This could be particularly crucial for countries which have a weak domestic competition policy.

The choice of exchange rate regime traditionally has been analyzed in the literature on optimum currency areas: MUNDELL has emphasized high labor/factor mobility as a prerequisite for fixing the exchange rate: a country can forego the exchange rate policy option if workers from high unemployment regions readily will move to low unemplyoment regions and find new jobs there. McKINNON has argued that a high share of tradables would suggest that the devaluation option is useless since devaluation will quickly raise almost all prices which will stimulate parallel wage increases – international price competitiveness thus cannot be improved by devaluation. KENEN has emphasized that a highly diversified country would find it relatively easy to live without the option of a devaluation since a diversified output and export structure implies that negative external random shocks and positive random shocks are likely to cancel out.

Having this standard set of arguments in mind we will proceed with our analysis where it is obvious that socialist countries were highly specialized in the socialist CMEA (Council of Mutual Economic Assistence). Labor mobility in the first stage of transition was low because social amenities were tied to the firm – from kindergartens to social security and firm-owned vacation camps; moreover, there was a structural excess demand for housing in most cities. The share of exports and imports in output was lower than in comparable countries of western Europe; here one can only compare countries of similar size where small countries are known to have very high export-GDP ratios (eg 2/3 for Belgium). Based on the above standard arguments from the optimum currency area literature the immediate conclusion is that one finds only weak arguments for fixed exchange rates. However, this is until here we have taken only a first glance at the problem.

Facing Transformation in a World of High Capital Mobility

With capital markets becoming more and more liberalized in the 1970s and 1980s in OECD countries and NICs, it became more difficult to maintain fixed exchange rates as the enormous amount of short term and long term capital flows make a rigid pegging of the exchange rate almost impossible: Central banks willing to defend the parity would have to accumulate enormous amounts of foreign exchange or accept large long term intervention commitments which might not look credible if they were to defend a parity which market participants consider as a disequilibrium value. The problem is reinforced by technological progress which tends to bring about long term reductions of information and transaction costs. Taking these arguments into account, as stated clearly in CORDEN (1993), one should not expect countries opening up to adopt any rigid pegging of the nominal exchange rate e.

Given the many initial domestic distortions and problems (eg monopolies, many state-owned firms, high external indebtedness, high budget deficits etc.) that one typically will find in transforming economies, including multiple exchange rates and black foreign exchange markets, it is only natural that economic opening up should go along with certain measures aiming at raising output and stabilizing the economy: liberalization of foreign exchange markets, banking reforms – including privatization and introduction of prudential supervision – and introduction of prudent macroeconomic policies, that is low budget deficits and an independent central bank committed to low inflation rates in the long term. Switching from state-administered socialist prices, which in many markets were set below market-clearing levels, to market clearing prices will entail a transitory boost in inflation, which cannot be avoided if a functional market economy is to be established; moreover, the tradables sector will have to adjust to relative world market prices which takes time (WELFENS, 1992). Labor and capital inputs also had to adjust accordingly in transforming economies of eastern Europe. Note that we disregard here the special case of the former GDR which was merged with the Federal Republic of Germany in 1990 and had very special circumstances since the

GDR currency was heavily appreciated in the context of monetary union and since 64 million West Germans were willing to pay enormous transfers – roughly $ 80 billions annually - for more than a decade (WELFENS, 1997b).

It is doubtful that a fundamental equilibrium exchange rate should be associated – as done often in the literature – with full employment and a balanced current account. Since trade increasinly is in financial services and since comparative advantage of a country could be related to the quality of its banking system in combination with the stability of the political system one could argue that a Switzerland-type economy naturally will have a long term current account deficit which mainly reflects net capital inflows. A similar argument could refer to the US and Euroland, respectively. The economic return on political stability and a competitive banking system is an improved terms of trade and real interest rates below the world market.

Given the fact that long term growth in any economy is not exceeding ten percent one can pragmatically derive the conclusion that with a given velocity of money the growth rate of the money supply should not exceed 10-12 % if price stability is to be achieved, but this is not easily achieved under distorted initial conditions. This reasoning takes into account the quantity equation in the form:

$M\,V(Y,i) = PY$

(1´) $g_M = g_P + g_Y$ under assumption that V is constant or has its steady state value (g denotes growth rates)

Postsocialist countries recorded very high inflation rates in the late 1980s and early 1990s, some even experienced currency substitution: The effective money supply M´ is given in the latter case by:

$M' = M + eM^*$

and hence

(2´) $g_{M'} = [M/M']\, g_M + [1-(M/M')]\, \{g_e + g_{M^*}\}$

where M is the domestic money supply, e the nominal exchange rate and M* the stock of foreign money circulating and being used for transaction purposes. Even if the growth rate of the nominal domestic money supply were zero and M* would be constant the effective money supply would still increase as long as there is an exchange rate depreciation. Switching from floating to an adequate crawling peg – indeed used by Poland and Hungary in a second transition stage - could be a strategic move to break expectations of accelerating nominal depreciations.

M is equal to H + eR*, where H is the domestic money supply component and R* the stock of foreign exchange reserves in our economy. A first challenge is to eliminate currency substitution which typically has occured as a consequence of hyperinflation and domestic financial repression, often including a black exchange rate market. Consequently, it is crucial to liberalize financial markets and to allow domestic banks to offer adequate yields on legal foreign exchange accounts. It also will be necessary to strictly control the domestic money supply – and hence the budget deficit assuming that a government dependent central bank used to cover deficits by printing money. A radical choice is to make the central bank politically independent and to eliminate H so that the domestic money stock is covered by foreign reserves. As poor countries have a tendency to rely on high imports it is most unlikely that there will be high current account surplusses which in turn would translate into high growth rates of foreign reserves and the money supply, respectively.

Economic Opening up, Balance of Payments and Trade

Given the initial situation of excess demand in many markets and the existence of other distortions a flexible exchange rate in the initial stage of transition is clearly needed. Once we have achieved a transitory equilibrium – still an incomplete equilibrium as there will be high unemployment rates at first – government has to decide whether if wants a fixed exchange rate regime or should stick to the flexible exchange rate. Since a major challenge of systemic transformation is economic opening up and expansion of trade, respectively, one should not forget that flexible exchange rates systematically avoid the problem of a balance of payments crisis and the protectionist tendencies typically observed in such a situation. Socialist countries were economies in which certain sectors, eg heavy industry and the military-industrial complex, were sheltered by government authorities; soft loans and priority allocation of inputs were characteristic here, and given the general lack of competition in socialist economies it is not difficult to understand that opening up in transition countries typically is associated with a strong potential protectionism. Having this in mind one can only recommend a high degree of exchange rate flexibility in the first stages of transformation.

An exception are the Visegrad countries to the extent that they are considered as early EU accession countries. The EU acquis communautaire imposes the principles of free trade in goods and services plus freedem of investment and free labor movement that prospects for EU membership reflect a strong institutional anchor for liberal trade; this holds the more if the country considered is a WTO member. In this respect the Visegrad countries seriously could consider fixed – but adjustable - exchange rates at some point. Russia, the Ukraine and many other countries in eastern Europe lack any similar institutional anchors and therefore should adopt a regime of flexible exchange rates for many years to come.

Disinflation, Sectoral Shifts and Exchange Rate Regime

Now assume that there is no institutional anchor for imposing a liberal trade regime; and there still is relatively high inflation. In such a situation many countries have considered to introduce a fixed exchange rate in order to signal that there will be a regime shift in monetary policy will. While fixing the exchange rate after a first transition stage might be considered as a useful element in a strategy designed at achieving low inflation rates by combining stability oriented monetary policy and fiscal austerity measures it is not necessary to maintain a fixed exchange rate in the long run. Having achieved low inflation rates government indeed might consider to switch back to flexible exchange rates.

Paradoxically, if initially low inflation rates can be combined with improved growth prospects the country – having fixed the exchange rate - might attract excessive capital inflows which would cause a strong expansion of the money supply growth and hence renewed inflation: In a large economy both the price of tradables and the price of nontradables will increase since any excess supply in the money market will be reflected in a temporary excess demand in both the tradables and the nontradables market. Assume that the production structure of the tradables sector reflects a specialization on those goods which face weak long term demand in the world market. This a worst case scenario since a real appreciation combined with unfavorable export spezialization is bound to lead to a rising current account deficit which ultimately will require a strong devaluation. In a small open economy – with tradables prices in domestic currency equal to the exchange rate times the exogenous world market price – only the nontradables pirces will go up, and this implies a relative price increase of nontradables so that production of tradables will fall; the result is a current account deficit (assuming an initially balanced current account position). As regards prospects for sustained high FDI inflows the rise of nontradables prices is bad news since industrial assets – including land and real estate used in the business community – will become more expansive. FDI in real terms therefore will slow down.

What happens with massive capital inflows in a setting of flexible exchange rates? Under flexible exchange rates there will a currency appreciation which will reduce tradable prices (reflecting arbitrage which will bring about P^T=e P^T* where P^T* is the world market price) in the medium term so that the relative price of tradables will fall, and this will discourage the export sector, rather the nontradables sector will expand. From the perspective of foreign investors the real appreciation of the currency makes acquiring industrial assets in the host country more expensive so that FDI inflows will reduce. So far the results are not really different from what we have seen in the fixed exchange rate case. The main difference will, however, refer to different impact on foreign debt. The appreciation in the flexible exchange rate setting means that the burden of foreign debt is reduced via an appreciation and this ultimately is a gain for the government budget and the taxpayer, respectively. From this perspective countries with considerable external debt could be inclined to favor flexible exchange rates because they assume that there will be a long term real appreciation; if the opposite would be shown in reality the flexible exchange rate system has serious consequnces. Note, however, that so far we always have argued that the (poor) country under consideration naturally will have FDI net inflows. This is a strong presumption, often poor countries with high foreign debt will be in a position where there is little hope for much capital inflow, including FDI.

Whether government budget deficits and foreign lending are sustainable mainly depends on economic growth, taxation and the real interest rate. Assume that the rate of return on public investment in eastern Europe is 20% and that the resulting economic growth is subject to a 25% tax rate then the country can sustainably finance all of this investment via borrowing if the real world interest rate is 5% (=0.2x0.25). The effective world interest rate is given by $r^*+(dq/dt)/q$ where q is eP^*/P, that is the real exchange rate. Moreover, we note that total investment must equal domestic savings plus public saving plus foreign saving – the latter being equal to the current account deficit. If the ability to finance a large current account would be affected by the exchange rate system a country wishing to accelerate development by a high investment-GDP ratio would opt in favor of that system. It is likely that a fixed exchange rate system would allow to mobilize higher overall savings relative to host country GDP than a flexible exchange rate system: The hypothesis is that a system of flexible exchange rate system will go along with more short term borrowing as international investors are concerned about the risk of strong exchang rate changes. This in turn would shorten average investment project´s time horizon which could imply lower growth to the extent that projects with very high productivity gains typically have to be long term and thus require long term investment and financing. This hypothesis should apply only for comparing two countries with low inflation rates so that we are not concerned here with effects from hyperinflation or capital flight.

For a stuctural net capital exporter – such as Russia or Romania - with a weak banking system and visible political instability (in Russia at least under president Yeltsin) the situation is different; flexible exchange rate make sense since rising demand for foreign exchange will bring about a strong depreciation which make industrial assets relatively cheap for foreign investors: Once the country combines privatiization, adequate infrastructure and labor market policies with flexible exchange rates this should lead to rising FDI inflows which counterbalance the portfolio capital outflows. Under fixed exchange rate the central bank – facing high demand for foreign exchange from people who want to transfer savings abroad – will quickly run out of foreign reserves and therefore will be forced to devalue strongly – and this is a new impulse for inflation. For a highly indebted country with high potential capital outflows the only alternative to a flexible exchang rate system seems to be a currency board; this is such a hard monetary regime that motivation for capital flight/high capital outflows should be rather weak. Note, however, that the initial coverage of the stock of domestic money can hardly be achieved without official long term foreign currency loans. A currency board is useful to the extent that it achieves low inflation rates and stimulates export promotion – a current account surplus is the only way to indirectly increase the domestic stock of money; Bulgaria, Bosnia and Estonia are examples of currency boards. Under such a regime strongly rising unit labor costs, typically as a consequence of high nominal wage increases, can be a serious problem since this will rapidly will lead to unemployment. As firms in the tradables sector cannot increase prices (remember that a small open economy is a price taker) excessive wage increases, that is wages growth above labor productivity growth will cause bankruptcies and laying off workers in the tradables sector. Hence a currency board should not be introduced if labor markets are not highly flexible and if trade unions are not supporting the currency board regime. A tax-based incomes policy which imposes high marginal income taxes on „excessive" wage increases could be useful to moderate wage demand.

The most crucial strategic challenge in a transforming economy – facing economic deterioration in the first stage – is to restore prospects for growth and this means to stimulate savings and investment in a new framework of competitive banking and competitive markets. Once there is economic growth, trade will expand and foreign direct investment inflows should occur; unfortunately, many transforming economies (and developing countries) never have achieved this status. FDI inflows then in turn should stimulate output growth so that per capita income will grow and this in turn will raise relative prices of nontradables in terms of tradables in accordance with the BALASSA hypothesis.

Opening up and Growth

Economic growth requires privatization and competiton plus reallocation of labor, namely that workers move from unprofitable low productivity firms and sectors into dynamic profitable firms. Moreover, a high investment-GDP ratio combined with a functional capital market plus FDI inflows are needed for achieving sustained growth. Opening up the economy will not only bring about opportunities for attracting FDI but also for realizing gains from specialization, economies of scale and product differentiation. Technology transfer via FDI and import of intermediate products also can help to raise output growth.

Absolute price levels of all output goods might increase if high growth raises the price of land and real estate. Again, the price of nontradables is likely to increase relative to that of tradables. To the extent that nontradables are an input into the production of tradables this will affect the quantity of tradables which can be exported by a small open economy which is a price taker in the world market as long as its firms are not leading innovators (eg case of Swiss pharmaceutical firms). Under this pressure a dynamic open economy will normally move up the technology ladder, that is drop the production of low quality products for which price competition is extreme in world markets. More technology intensive Schumpeterian product groups will be included in the export basket, and those products can fetch higher prices in world markets including a Schumpeterian premium, typical for innovative products. As regards Schumpeterian dynamics countries in eastern Europe are different; countries which are richly endowed with skilled labor – such as Hungary, the Czech Republic or Poland – could try to increase the knowledge intensity of exports products in the long run. Adequate government promotion of private research and development is crucial here. Countries with strong Schumpeterian dynamics will find it relatively easy to cope with a moderst rise of the real echange rate.Note that the experience from Asian countries suggests that government R&D expenditures in a first stage (over a decade or so) mainly will strengthen ability of domestic firms to imitate and emulate technologies from abroad, that is diffusion-enhancing policies are important. In a more long term development stage Asian NICs have become significant innovators themselves as is obvious from the number of patent applications at the European Patent Agency or the US Patent Office.

In the world of liberalized capital flows and relatively free trade the polar cases are no longer fixed versus flexible exchange rates. Rather, the question is, how much exchange rate flexibility should one try to achieve at what stage of development? For regions with very close trade and investment links the option of a currency board or of full monetary union seems to be more attractive in a world of globalization than it was in previous periods. Monetary union has the advantage that each member country somehow will be represented in monetary decision-making. A currency board is a dependency solution in which a country surrenders its monetary sovereignty in a rather passive way. The advantage of establishing a currency board in a country with a long record of political instability and high inflation is that it creates within a very short period a new stability oriented monetary (and fiscal) regime which stimulates savings, investment and capital inflows. To some extent a currency board based on the US dollar or the Euro is similar to a strict gold standard. As the gold standard developed over time many countries did not fully cover extra mony supply with gold or they reduced the gold coverage ratio; also not all gold inflows were allowed to translate into an expansion of the money supply. With this in mind one might suggest that after many years of a currency board the central bank could introduce a more flexible currency board; such flexibility should be limited and fully transparent for market participants, otherwise reputation of the central bank will be seriously impaired. Massive capital outflows or capital flight and economic stagnation would be likely results from this.

A currency board such as those adopted in Bulgaria – based on full coverage of national currency by DM/Euro reserves - or Estonia (or Argentina in Latin America) can help to import creditibility of monetary policy in an initially totally uncredible and distorted monetary environment. Whether a currency board, however, is an optimal monetary regime for the long term, is an open question.

Any closed economy which is opening up to the world economy must decide which exchange rate regime it wants to adopt. In principle it can peg – with a more or less narrow parity band - the exchange rate strictly to one country or to a basket of countries; or it can chose full or limited exchange rate flexibility.

Fully fixed exchange rates worldwide have the advantage of minimzing transaction costs for international trade and capital flows. This advantage, however, comes at some costs since the exchange rate cannot be used to compensate a negative external shock. A typcial case is that the world demand for the country´s exports are reducing so that – assuming initial balanced current account – the current account will turn negative. This implies a twin problem of internal disequilibrium, that is unemployment because of reduced aggregate demand, and an external disequilibrium since exports of goods and services exceed imports. This implies an excess demand for foreign exchange so that the currency will depreciate. Such a development would solve the problems since depreciation raises import prices and makes exports more profitable: Net exports and hence output and employment will increase (under standard elasticity assumptions, that is the modified Marshall Lerner condition).

What is the relationsship between capital flows, growth and exchange rate regimes? Short term capital inflows are believed to make transition counries and NICs vulnerable to external shocks in the sense that world interest rate shocks or changes in political sentiments could cause a sudden reversal of capital flows. Rapid capital outflows normally go along with sharp increases in nominal and real interest rates plus a real depreciation. Would it be better not to have fully liberalized capital flows in an early stage of transition and thus deny people the alternative of relying on foreign financial services?

KRAY (1998) argued that capital account liberalization has not shown any negative impact on growth or growth volatility in a sample of developing countries and NICs. Even if this result would be robust one must raise the question whether not the more important question is whether early capital liberalization will not lead to high unemployment rates and stagnation in countries which have failed to adopt adequate banking reforms, prudential supervision and fiscal policies from the outset. A cross country regression is not very useful if Poland, Bulgaria, Russia or Brazil or India would like to have an answer to the question: What is the adequate sequencing of external liberalization and the adequate sequencing of exchange rate regimes? Moreover, an early comprehensive capital account liberalization is likely to lead to serious problems when capital flows are reversed, and then the IMF typically will step in – the country will lose the little political degree of freedem it has, and this is bad for nurturing political responsibility. From the perspective of international bank early comprehensive liberalization might be desirable just for this reason: With the IMF engaged in conditional loans future government policy is easy to anticipate (paradoxically, from a US perspective it is only fortunate that the IMF was not existing in the 19th century because the US would hardly have achieved independence from Great Britain had the IMF already existed). The evidence from the Asian crisis points to some useful measures imposed and encouraged by the IMF, but the overall picture is not really clear (LANE et al., 1999).

Unlimited exchange rate flexibility also comes at some costs, because it raises international transaction costs and hence impairs trade growth provided that exchange rate flexibility translates periodically into high exchange rate volatility. If international capital flows are rather volatile exchange rate volatility will be high? From a theoretical perspective the likelihood of high exchange rate volatility depends much on the degree of instability of monetary policies on the one hand, on the other hand the divergence of adjustment speed in goods markets – with slow adjustment speeds – and financial markets – with an ever increasing adjustment speed – plays a role. At this point one should note that the size of a country plays a crucial role here. A large economy such as the US or Euroland – with most trade within the country – should be able to live with high exchange rate volatility much better than a smaller economy which is not only more dependent on external trade but also more specialized and therefore faces a lower possibility that adverse exchange rate shocks are combined with positive technology shocks in expanding sectors of the economy.

Moreover, there is empirical evidence in UNCTAD (1993) that high exchange rate volatility (could occur in a flexible exchange rate regime but also under fixed exchange rates with strongly changing international inflation differentials leading to large real exchange rate swings) will reduce global foreign direct investment which in turn will impair the worldwide diffusion of knowledge – global output growth thus is impaired by excessive exchange rate flexibility. While FDI abroad could in principle serve as insurance against an appreciation of the exporting country and its MNCs´ potential interest in vertical international integration, a volatile real exchange rate is working like capital outflow barriers. Looking from the perspective of a capital rich country, the empirical evidence from UNCTAD suggests that the latter effect dominates the former. WELFENS/JUNGMITTAG (1997) found empirical evidence that in the period of the European Monetary System intra-EU exchange rate volatility had reduced investment in Germany and the Netherlands. This implies that switching to the Eurozone should raise the investment-GDP ratio in Euroland. It may not necessarily do the same in Germany and the Netherlands since multinational firms in both countries might want to raise the share of output of subsidiaries within Euroland given the fact that fully exploiting regional intra-Euroland cost advantages is becoming more crucial in a more transparent and integrated Euro zone.

A serious potential problem with fixed exchange rates is, of course, that undesirable real exchange rate changes will be realized as sustained international inflation differentials occur. The simplest way to avoid this problem, that is the problem of a real appreciation, is a currency union, the option realized by Euroland countries. For these countries this could – assuming a noninflationary monetary union - indeed make sense, because trade is mainly intra-Euroland(EU) trade, and also because FDI in the EU is dominantly intra-EU foreign direct investment. Moreover, the Euro-related impulses for integration of financial markets should raise competition in financial markets and help to improve the braedth of markets so that real interest rates should indeed fall once and for all. This will have a redistribution effect in favor of sectors with net debt, that is, government, the enterprise sector and households with a mortgage. Less exchange rate flexibility will come at low opportunity cost if monetary integration contributes to higher nominal wage flexibility – a case for which one can state pros and cons in Europe (ADDISON/WELFENS, 1998).

Even if a country cannot realize inflation preferences above Euroland average and cannot devaluate in periods in which it would like to improve price competitiveness more than Euroland partners vis-à-vis the dollar area, the benefits of low inflation and stable regional real exchange rates – direct welfare gains and indirect output plus wealth gains – should tilt rational choice towards currency union. For the UK and Denmark, two countries with still much extra-EU trade and potential ability to achieve low inflation rates by national monetary policy, the non-Euro option might be defendable. However, if real interest rates in the UK (and Denmark) should stay above those in Euroland in the long term – while not reflecting extraordinary output growth – the economic arguments in favor of staying out the Euro zone are doubtful. From an east European perspective the case of Euro zone membership becomes more convincing over time as progress with EU eastern enlargement should stimulate both trade of accession countries with Euroland and encourage higher EU FDI outflows towards prospective EU countries from eastern Europe.

As long as there is no clear argument in favor of Euroland membership, one will have to consider the issue of fixed versus floating exchange rates. Moreover, countries which initially pursued a peg against a currency basket, say DM/Euro and US dollar, will have to decide in the course of time how the weights in the basket should be changed (normally raising the share of the DM/Euro as the regional breakdown of trade is shifting in favor of a higher share of trade with the EU and Euroland, respectively). Finally, the government will have to consider whether not switching to a floating dollar exchange rate combined with fixing the exchange rate vis-à-vis the Euro – in the sense of a fixed but adjustable rate – is adequate. If this is realized the country has decided in favor of a certain exchange rate flexibility which could be calculated on the basis of trade weights.

The above reasoning suggests that there must be some optimum degree of exchange rate flexibility f* which in principle can be achieved both in a regime of fixed exchange rates, namely by frequent adequate devaluations of the home (or the foreign) currency in certain time intervals; or in a system of flexible exchange rates by limited depreciation and appreciation stages in the course of time. The main problem with flexible exchange rates is that there might be massive overshooting or magnification effects which imply large real exchange rate shifts that go beyond long term equilibrium requirements.

A Simple Model of Opening up in the Presence of Foreign Direct Investment

Exchange rate regimes are often discussed only with respect to trade issues. We will argue that in the era of economic globalization – with foreign direct investment (FDI) increasing fast – FDI aspects have to be considered too. Moreover, a two sector perspective which includes both tradables and nontradables (eg services, construction) is considered as adequate. The familiar MacDougall diagramm is shown for the tradables sector in country I and country II, where the initial allocation of capital at home (country I) is K_o and for country II K^*_o (see point F and G, respectively). Initially, the real interest rate r is higher in country I (r_o) than abroad ($r_o{}^*$). As capital is mobile both nationally and internationally FDI inflows in the tradables sector – as assumed here – will lead to equilibrium point E in panel a) where we have a uniform marginal product of capital at home and abroad. For simplicity we assume that country II has no nontradables sector.

Since after opening up the real interest rate has fallen in country I (r is equal to $r_2=r_2^*$) the marginal product must also fall in the nontradables sector. The profit-maximizing capital stock in that sector is larger than initially, that is K^N instead of $K^N o$ – hence nontradables output will increase. A higher capital stock in the N-sector either could be realized through the use of some of the new capital goods produced in the tradables sector which at a given savings rate implies a current account deficit; or all or part of the increase in the capital stock in the N sector is realized via FDI inflows into this sector. A third possibility is that part of the capital goods employed in the T-sector are used for expanding the capital stock in the N-sector – which then implies higher FDI inflows into the tradables sector. Note that there might be positive technology spillover effects into the N sector through cumulated FDI inflows into the T sector. This would imply an outward shift of the marginal product of capital schedule in the N sector (not shown here).

Fig. C7: Fig.: Foreign Direct Investment and Opening up in a Two-Sector Model

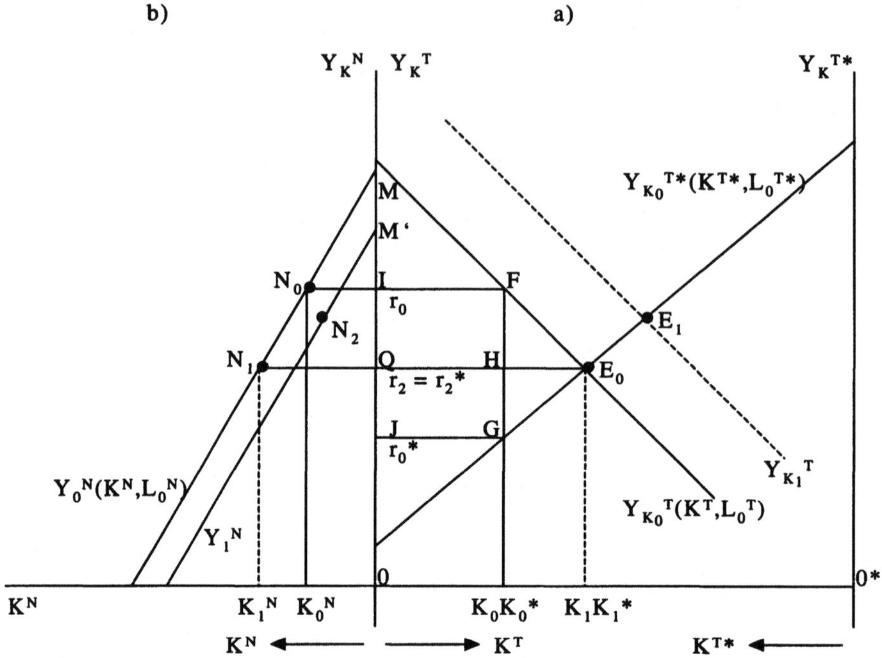

Whatever the way of expanding the capital stock employed in the N-sector the output in this sector will increase – the area under the Y^No curve (note the relevant capital input) is the output in the N-sector. However, with given domestic nontradables demand this cannot be an equilibrium situation. There will be an increase in GNP, namely by the area FHE so that there will be a small increase in both demand for tradables and nontradables. In a situation of an excess supply in the nontradables sector – as assumed here - there will be unemployment in this sector, that is the marginal product of capital curve in the N sector *(Y^No) will shift towards the origin as less workers will be employed than initially ($Y^N{}_1$). If these workers can easily transfer to the tradables sector – the case of a geographically small country – the medium term effect of economic opening up in country I is that the marginal product of the capital curve in the tradables sector is shifted to the right so that there will be a new equilibrium point E_1 which implies even higher FDI inflows into the tradables sector and a higher tradables output. Output in the N sector also will have to adjust as the marginal product of capital has increased.

FDI inflows into east European economies will be determined by domestic market size – especially with respect to FDI in the N sector – and to cost advantages in the case of tradable products. Expected profits are, of course, also important and here the exchange rate plays a natural role. A real depreciation of the currency means that foreigners can acquire capital more easily and it could stimulate net exports eQ/P^* $(X(eP/P^*,...))$ so that profits – evaluated in terms of investor's currency – could increase; note that Q stands here for nominal profits. A depreciation has two opposing effects, namely reducing profits evaluated in investor's currency and raising nominal profits in local currency due to higher real exports X.

Strategic Aspects

Many governments in postsocialist accession countries of eastern Europe are eager to fix exchange rates vis-a-vis the Euro, sooner rather than later. Fixing the exchange rate can, however, cause serious disadvantages if this is done too early – in a rather large economy or in a group of small economies (remember that EU eastern enlargement is comprised of two five-country groups). A typical motivation for fixing the exchange rate is to borrow credibility from abroad, mainly by fixing the exchange rate to a foreign currency with low inflation rate and a high reputation of the central bank. By doing this, it should be possible to achieve both low inflation rates and avoid a high risk premium in national and international bond markets.

Typical problems which often occur in a system of fixed exchange rates, however, are:

- monetary policy is not as stability oriented as abroad so that through higher inflation a real appreciation will be realized which dampens net exports and growth, but also will impair the inflow of foreign direct investment – again impairing growth;
- for political reasons nominal devaluations occur too late compared to the natural goal of avoiding a real appreciation, and since devaluation is kind of postponed it will be rather large (reflecing cumulated international inflation differentials);
- if in a three-country world country A has pegged the exchange rate to B which in turn has a floating rate via C an extended period of appreciation of the B currency – reflecting cyclical or structural factors – will undermine the global competitiveness of country A. If currency b is appreciated because of higher Schumpeterian innovation and growth dynamics in country B while country A has not an acceleration of innovation dynamics country A should devaluate. This, however, is unpopular for various reasons.

Small countries often peg their exchange rate to the dominant trading partner which should facilitate trade and encourage investment in the tradables sector. In eastern Europe there are several small countries, but also some larger economies, such as Poland, Ukraine or Russia. Unfortunately the term small economy is not really clear in Economics. It has the meaning (i) that the country is too small to affect world market prices, and in this sense all countries in eastern Europe, except Russia – in some natural resources – are small countries; (ii) a second notion is that a small country is one without geographical relocation costs of production factors. A country which is large in a geographical sense could be small in the latter sense if there is an outstanding infrastructure which can be used at subsidized prices (eg highways in most OECD countries).

Take a look at the first group of accession countries. Poland is a rather large country, Estonia, Slovenia, Hungary and the Czech Republic are small open economies. Estonia is a pure small open economy in the sense that it is so small that it resembles a neoclassical market with very low spatial adjustment costs; eg if for some external shock resources would have to shift from the tradables sector to the nontradables sector or vice versa this should not lead to long term unemployment as every worker faces low intersectoral mobility costs. If there is heterogenous labor in a setup where skilled labor and unskilled labor are used in different intensities in both sectors there could be temporary unemployment if we assume that unemployed skilled workers can find new jobs in the other sector only after some time-consuming skill upgrading (at positive marginal costs).

An adverse external shock to the tradables sector cannot be compensated by a devaluation if the accession country has pegged its exchange rate. However, in a rather small economy, labor can easily be reallocated from the tradables sector to the nontradables sector. Given a fall of tradables this could be the case of a Keynesian fiscal expansion which should mainly fall on the nontradables sector. Note, however, that this will raise P^N/P^T which impairs long term price competitiveness to the extent that nontradables are inputs in production in tradabales. An alternative scenario is an exogenous decrease in the nontradables demand. Again, we assume that in a very small country workers could move from the nontradables to the tradables sector. For the case of a small open economy – in the textbook sense this means a country whose firms are pricetakers in world markets – one might assume that exports indeed could be raised without problems. This assumption, however, is doubtful if the same problem (eg a slump in construction industry or industrial services) is, at the same time, affecting several small economies which have specialized along similar lines. Taken together they will be able to raise exports only at falling terms of trade, that is in the presence of a real depreciation.

In the course of economic catching up of accession countries one should expect that the inflation rate will be slightly higher than Euroland average if the exchange rate is pegged to the Euro. The reason for this is associated with the BALASSA argument that with rising per capita income the relative price ratio of tradables to nontradables will fall. If due to arbitrage the domestic price of tradables $P^T = eP^{T*}$ where e is the nominal exchange rate and P^{T*} (* indicates foreign variables) the world price of tradables and if the overall price level at home is $P=P^T \exp ß\, P^T \exp (1-ß)$ and $P^*=P^{T*}$ - so that for simplicity country II has only tradables - we have the following equation for domestic inflation (where ß denotes the share of nontradables in the basket of all goods consumed):

(3) $g_P = ßg_{PN} + (1-ß)[\, g_e + g_{PT*}] = g_{PT*} + ßg_{PN/PT} + (1-ß)\, g_e$

Under strictly fixed exchange rates the percentage change g_e of the nominal exchange rate is zero. The domestic inflation rate then, is equal to the inflation rate g_{PT*} if there is no relative price effect in the sense of $g_{PN/PT}=0$. With economic catching up, however, there typically is a relative increase of P^N/P^T which often is associated with increasing land and real estate and construction prices, respectively. Applying the marginal productivity rule of factor reward, this relative price increase indeed could reflect a technological rate of progress in labor productivity in the nontradables sector (the services sector) which is lower than in the tradables sector. All this is well known as the Balassa argument and implies that an enlarged Euro zone will be characterized by peripheral catching-up economies where inflation is structurally above the Euroland average. Under flexible exchange rate, the typical equilibrium relative price shift P^N/P^T also could be brought about by a nominal appreciation so that with constant nominal nontradable prices the absolute price of tradables would fall. Assume a given world market price of tradables: any nominal appreciation will translate into falling absolute prices of tradables unless there are monopoly distortions in the tradables markets. In a small open economy this normally should play no significant role, in a large economy – such as Poland (or Russia or the Ukraine) – this could play some role.

The conclusion is that in a purely neoclassical country without distortions both fixed and flexible exchange rates could bring about the BALASSA effect of a rising relative price ratio PN/PT in the course of rising per capita income. From a welfare analytical point of view the rise of the inflation rate in the presence of a fixed exchange rate is not desirable since the real demand for money is reduced by inflation and higher nominal interest rates, respectively. From this perspective a flexible exchange rate is indeed adequate.

For a geographically large economy such as Poland labor certainly is not perfectly mobile in space. If Poland would, therefore, face an adverse demand shock in the tradables sector, it is doubtful that labor could easily be relocated to the nontradables sector and that government – facing the Maastricht debt and deficit criteria – could easily finance a fiscal expansion package designed to promote expansion in the nontradables or the tradables sector.

While the size of the economy and its potential for catching-up – the international per capita income divergence – naturally have to be considered when it comes to the question of fixed versus flexible exchange rates, one has also to focus on geographic location. The gravity equation suggests that exports from country i to j positively depends on output in i and j, but negatively on distance. For countries with close proximity to high income regions – eg Poland is close to Germany and the EU, but Romania and Bulgaria (with a currency board) in the second accession group are not – it should be easier to increase exports in a period of declining nontradables demand than for countries far away from major potential trading partners. This implies that countries far away from major trading countries need more exchange rate flexibility than those which are closer. Therefore it holds that size, per capita income, the role of initial distortions and relative geographical location crucially influence the decision of fixed versus flexible exchange rates.

One should emphasize that the gravity equation has also been applied to foreign direct investment (FDI) which implies that opportunity to attract higher FDI inflows and hence government ability to compensate negative demand shocks - to the tradables or the nontradables sector – is positively influenced by proximity to rich countries; and proven ability to attract significant FDI inflows at all. With a devaluation government could not only improve the export sector´s growth due to the fact that in an international perspective relative wages have fallen, it also could hope to attract higher (net) FDI inflows along the reasoning of FROOT/STEIN (1991). They have argued that normalized FDI inflows will be increased in a setting with imperfect capital markets if there is a devaluation or depreciation in the host country. Since this improves the ability of firms from major FDI source countries to successfully outbid domestic rivals interested in taking over a certain firm, foreign firms effectively finds firms in the host country cheaper they will increasingly engage in international mergers and acquisitions.

Fig. C8: Main Aspects of Exchange Rate Regimes

Domestic Distortions (eg monopolies versus competition, flexible wages versus rigid wages)	Size of Country: Large versus Small (includes aspects of diversification of output)
Proximity to Major FDI Source Countries/Large Trading Partner	External Indebtedness/ Political Instability

Under flexible exchange rates any prolonged depreciation should stimulate higher FDI inflows assuming that there is at least some overshooting so that firms acquire assets ideally at depressed prices and later record some capital gains in terms of source country currency units. Under fixed exchange rates devaluation could occur in principle but in the context of a strict currency union this would be ruled out. Postsocialist accession countries fixing the exchange rate, vis-a-vis the

Euro, would have to develop a Schumpeterian FDI promotion policy in periods of adverse demand shocks. Government expenditures would have to be raised in order to attract at a given exchange rate higher FDI inflows through higher infrastructure endowment or increasing R&D promotion which could be partly taylored to directly benefit foreign MNC subsidiaries in technology intensive sectors. Countries which are small and far away from big international markets should have flexible exchange rates. Large countries with proven ability to attact high per capita inflows might survive adverse demand shocks even with rather rigid exchange rates.

Beyond these arguments it is useful to recall the classical arguments from optimum currency area theory, namely that a high degree of diversification in output and exports is relatively easy to reconcile with fixed exchange rates – more likely to apply to large countries than to highly specialized small economies - as is a high share of tradables in overall output. The latter argument does not really mean that small economies should be more inclined to fixed exchange rates than small ones. While it is true that the export-GDP ratio of a small economy is typically higher than in a large economy the overall share of tradables in GDP should be equal in both countries. The point is, in the large economy the share of domestic trade tradables is larger than in the small economy. Based on the diversification argument a large economy should find it easier to live with a fixed exchange rate.

As the example of Russia in 1997/98 as a country with natural resources, that is oil and gas, dominating export revenues has shown, it is especially doubtful to have a fixed exchange rate if exports are very much concentrated on a few products with very volatile world market prices. Rapidly falling oil prices contributed to the August 1998 ruble crisis and the sharp devaluation. The doubts about fixing the exchange rate here indeed is consistent with the Kenen criterion of optimum currency areas where the argument is that a country with a rather diversified ouput and export structure could indeed give up the policy option of exchange rate adjustment.

The worst case of fixing the exchange rate would be a small economy, with an inflation-prone central bank, which is far away from one of the leading global economic centers, eg countries in the former CIS with minor trade links with Russia, or countries in Africa. Even if such a country could establish a politically independent central bank with a stability-oriented central bank (this implicitly assumes that government can achieve a low budget deficit ratio) fixing the exchange rate rigidly would hardly bring considerable benefits. Government could combine a policy of selective promotion of inward FDI from that source country which is considered to be most likely to be the dominant trading partner in the future. This is to say that the benefits of chosing fixed or flexible exchange rates can hardly be assessed without specifying which government policies are adopted and which size and location aspects are relevant.

To summarize we can argue that large economies with few domestic distortions and close proximity to large FDI source countries or major trading partner face limited risks when pursuing a policy of fixed exchange rates. Much will depend on setting the initial equilibrium exchange rate right. A small open economy also could adopt a fixed exchange rate regime provided that the export-GDP ratio is large – which is natural for small open economies – and that the central bank is committed to a stability-oriented monetary policy. Given the increasing role of international capital flows and the large divergence of adjustment speeds in goods and financial markets one should have a certain minimum exchange rate flexibility: In a fixed exchange rate regime this will imply relatively broad parity bands, in a system of flexible exchange rates one might have to avoid extreme depreciations – not in line with purchasing power parity – because massive protectionist tendencies would occur otherwise.

4. Summary and Conclusions

It will be difficult to achieve a consistent policy mix in Euroland where the ECB and the ECOFIN have to cooperate in the field of exchange rate policy. Euroland will need exchange rate flexibility vis-à-vis the US dollar and other currencies. While Euroland could live with considerable dollar exchange rate fluctuations, third countries might find big shifts more difficult to accept. A benign neglect attitude of Euroland would not be adequate in a period of economic globalization, but the reduced post-1999 EU dependency on imports and exports could contribute to such an attitude. A long-term broadly defined PPP range for the dollar exchange rate could be useful for stabilizing expectations of market participants. However, a (modified) PPP range can be defined adequately only after international portfolio adjustments – using the new Euro options – have been made, possibly bringing a dollar depreciation. A once-and-for-all dollar depreciation is warranted by the existence of dollar surplus holdings in EU countries and the incentives for developing countries to decrease the share of dollar holdings in official exchange reserve holdings.

Early entry of east European accession countries in ERM II – or even the Euro group – is quite inadequate since this would impair the economic catching-up process. Relative exchange rate stability can be achieved by credible stability-oriented ECB policies and some coordination with the US Fed. Exchange rate policy is not suitable for reducing unemployment rates in Europe; rather a credible ECB policy could nurture EU capital markets and thereby contribute to growth and employment (WELFENS/WOLF, 1997). Special attention should be devoted to global crisis management where Euroland could launch an initiative to strengthen the role of the Bank of International Settlements. The BIS could be encouraged to send out special early warnings to countries likely to face major financial problems, and the government of the respective country would have to answer a standardized set of questions which would mandatorily be published if the country's devaluation rates exceeded 25 % within a year. The conditional publication requirements should make sure that warned countries give a true picture of the situation in the answering letter. The 25% threshold would be intended to encourage adequate timely policy measures.

A rather difficult situation for Euroland would emerge if there were a strong Euro appreciation in the starting period. This points to the need for urgent measures in labor market reforms in (most) EU countries. EMU should help to reduce exchange rate variability (including for the dollar) and thus contribute to higher global FDI and growth in OECD countries. The reduction of the money supply variability in the EMU area to one-half of the DM variability would add about ½ percentage point to the long term investment-output ratio in Germany (JUNGMITTAG/WELFENS, 1998). This indicates that EMU might have considerable benefits especially if monetary supply growth is efficiently controlled. Therefore the topic of monetary policy strategies will rank high on the ESCB´s agenda. Visible success in controlling inflation in countries where the central bank has adopted a direct inflation target (eg UK, Switzerland, Sweden, New Zealand, Canada) might intensify discussions at the ECB. However, some of these countries have shown a high volatility of interest rates which might be a high price for a strategy of direct inflation targetting. Moreover, one may wonder whether a direct output inflation target is not strategically insufficient as future output prices and asset price shifts are not taken into account. If money demand stability should have weakened – making it more difficult to pursue a monetary target – money supply targets would become less convincing. In a situation of more financial innovations – in Euroland partly stimulated by intensified competition – this indeed could become a serious problem. So there are new research topics on the future research agenda.

Appendix C

Tab. C1: Main Features of International Debt Securities Issues[1]

By instruments, residence, currency and type of issuer In billions of US dollars (or %)	1992	1993	1994	1995	1996	1997	Stocks at end-1997
Total net issues (a)	149.9	189.0	256.5	268.2	543.4	595.9	3,542.2
Money market instruments[2]	12.1	- 6.3	3.3	17.4	41.1	19.8	183.8
Bonds and notes[2]	137.9	195.2	253.3	250.9	502.3	576.0	3,358.3
Developed countries	114.0	123.0	184.7	198.7	363.3	394.1	2,604.4
Europe[3]	92.6	137.9	151.9	148.2	212.0	223.7	1,531.5
Japan	- 3.4	- 45.8	- 27.7	- 29.4	- 17.6	- 32.7	156.5
United States	16.9	10.2	37.2	62.2	144.9	185.4	614.2
Canada	10.5	19.0	16.8	9.1	9.8	9.1	187.9
Offshore centers	0.0	5.2	35.3	33.8	74.6	91.6	323.7
Other countries	12.7	24.7	27.9	24.0	80.4	79.7	297.8
International institutions	23.1	36.1	8.6	11.7	25.0	30.4	316.4
US dollar (b)	58.1	28.9	67.3	70.2	262.8	336.5	1,569.3
EU currencies (c)	84.1	111.2	96.8	98.0	175.3	199.0	1,191.8
Yen (d)	9.1	29.3	87.5	83.6	85.1	34.2	462.0
Other currencies	- 1.4	19.6	4.9	16.4	20.2	26.2	319.1
US dollar in % (b/a)	38.75	15.29	26.29	26.17	48.36	56.47	44.30
EU currencies in % (c/a)	56.10	58.84	37.74	36.54	32.26	33.39	33.65
Yen in % (d/a)	6.07	15.50	34.11	31.17	15.66	5.74	13.04
Financial institutions[4]	42.9	51.8	138.5	170.7	351.0	368.2	1,605.5
Public sector[5]	82.7	130.8	103.3	74.0	121.4	101.8	1,067.0
Corporate issuers	24.4	6.5	14.7	23.6	71.0	125.9	869.7
Memorandum items:							
Stand-alone international bonds	109.5	116.8	116.3	75.8	278.3	292.2	2,469.0
Bonds issued under EMTN programs	11.0	38.4	86.9	104.4	195.9	215.8	604.9

[1]Flow data for international bonds; for money market instruments and notes, changes in amounts outstanding, excluding exchange rate valuation effects.
[2]Excluding notes issued by non-residents in the domestic market.
[3]Excluding Eastern Europe.
[4]Commercial banks and other financial institutions.
[5]Governments, state agencies and international institutions.
Source: Based on BIS (1998), 68th Annual Report

Tab. C2: Currency Composition of EU Countries' Foreign Exchange Reserves, %

	End 1995	ECU-US$ Swaps included as US$, End 1995
US$	39.9	58.0
Yen	5.3	6.1
SwFr	0.3	0.3
ECUs	23.6	-
EU Currencies	26.6	30.7
—DM	20.2	23.3
—FFr	3.4	4.0
—UK£	2.7	3.1
—NlG	0.3	0.3
Other	4.3	5.0

Source: Brookes (1998)

Tab. C3: Foreign Exchange Reserves at the ECB

	Non-EU Foreign Exchange Reserves ($bn)*	Share of ECB Capital (%)	Foreign Exchange Contribution to ECB ($bn)	"Surplus" Foreign Exchange Reserves ($bn)
Germany	68.9	31.0	14.0	54.8
France	14.6	21.1	9.5	5.0
Italy	32.2	19.0	8.6	23.6
Spain	46.3	11.2	5.1	41.3
Netherlands	15.1	5.4	2.4	12.7
Belgium/Lux	9.7	3.9	1.7	8.0
Austria	13.2	3.0	1.4	11.9
Portugal	9.6	2.5	1.1	8.5
Finland	5.7	1.8	0.8	4.9
Ireland	4.5	1.1	0.5	4.0
Total	219.7	100	45.1	174.6

* Estimates for non-EU foreign exchange reserves at end-1997

Source: Brookes (1998)

Tab. C4: Gold Reserves at the ECB

	Gold Reserves (tonnes)	Share of ECB Capital (%)	Gold Contribution to ECB*	"Surplus" Gold (tonnes)
Germany	3,700	31.0	354	3,346
France	3,182	21.1	241	2,941
Italy	2,592	19.0	216	2,376
Spain	608	11.2	128	480
Netherlands	1,052	5.4	62	990
Belgium/Lux	309	3.9	44	265
Austria	418	3.0	34	384
Portugal	625	2.5	29	596
Finland	62	1.8	20	42
Ireland	14	1.1	13	1
Total	12,562	100	1,141	11,421

*Assumption is that 20% of a country's overall contribution will be in gold.

Source: Brookes (1998)

Tab. C5: Currency Composition of Developing Countries' Foreign Exchange Reserves, %

	End 1996
US$	62.5
Yen	6.2
SwFr	1.4
ECUs	-
EU Currencies	17.5
—DM	10.6
—FFr	1.5
—UK£	4.9
—NlG	0.5
Other	12.4

Source: Brookes (1998)

Tab. C6: The Euro Economy and Financial Markets, $bn

	GDP[1]	Share of World Trade, % [2]	Govern-ment Bond Market[3]	Internat. Bonds Out-standing [4]	Internat. Bond Issuance[4]	Equity Market[5]
EU	7333	20.1	2545	814	109	3699
-EU(11)	5792	18.6	1934	610	85	1955
US	6316	16.1	2142	861	136	7227
Japan	3316	8.5	1057	330	21	2643

[1] 1996 real GDP using 1990 PPP exchange rates and prices.

[2] 1996 exports plus imports as a share of world exports plus imports excluding trade among EMU-11 countries.

[3] Market capitalization, March 1998. Data for Finland, Portugal, Greece, Ireland and Luxembourg are not available.

[4] Bonds issued by non-residents in 1996 in currency of the country. Data for Ireland and Greece are not available.

[5] Market capitalization, June 1997. Data for Portugal, Greece and Luxembourg are not available.

Source: Brookes (1998)

Tab. C7: Currency Shares of Global Holdings of Foreign Exchange Reserves

	Actual	Optimal	Optimal With Euro
US$	74	38	34
Yen	9	23	18
DM	17	39	48

Source: IMF

Tab. C8: Wages and Productivity in Euroland

Country	Productivity (A)	Labor cost (B)	B / A	Unemployment (standardized)	Patents
G (West)	100	100	1	8.3	7796*
(Ex-GDR)	60.4	74.4	1.23	15.7	
F	95.3	95.6	1	12.4	3312
I	85.3	79.9	0.94	12.1	1383
SP	62.0	66.9	1.08	20.8	144
NL	85.4	94.4	1.11	5.2	1141
B	97.6	107.6	1.1	9.2	379
AU	90.9	89.5	0.98	4.4	390
FL	81.4	93.8	1.15	14.0	321
IR	69.5	71.8	1.03	10.2	51
PG	34.5	37.4	1.08	6.8	5
UK	71.7	68.0	0.95	7.1	2081

A: nominal GDP per person employed as % of West Germany

B: gross compensation per employee as % of West Germany

* East and West-Germany together

Source: Siebert, H. (1998), European Patent Agency (1997), Annual Report, own calculations

Tab. C9: Specialization* of Selected OECD Countries in R&D Intensive Technology Field with High Patent Growth Rates

	Growth**	USA	Japan	Germany	France	UK	Switzerland	Canada	Sweden	Italy	Netherlands
telecommunication	13,6	10	-3	-34	-7	17	-75	50	70	-67	18
turbines	10,6	-8	-74	-40	87	8	83	-84	-7	-96	-52
railways (vehicles)	8,5	-74	-41	67	9	-67	58	-22	-19	0	-26
paper machinery	7,6	-4	-88	28	-71	-43	-54	30	85	-41	-62
automotive	6,7	-47	-14	57	35	-31	-84	-71	-12	10	-56
medical instruments	6,6	46	-80	-38	-36	-7	38	-64	32	-20	-29
advanced electronical products	6,4	-18	46	1	-21	-18	-52	42	-52	-44	48
power distribution	6,4	-20	8	16	34	-23	-27	-53	13	-7	-36
agrochemicals	6,1	35	-59	0	-3	5	22	52	-53	-13	-69
medical electronics	5,8	42	-31	-47	-64	-9	-48	-19	10	-65	35

* Specialisation: relative patent share in 1995–1997

** Average annual growth of EPA patent applications in period 1989–1997 (in percent)

Source: FhG-ISI, Karlsruhe

The Euro and Financial Market Integration

With the convergence process imposed by the Maastricht criteria, nominal and real interest rates in Italy, Spain and some other Euroland candidates/countries have fallen and average maturities of government debt have increased. The first effect is a massive windfall gain for government budget, above all in Italy where the interest payment/GDP ratio fell by roughly three percentage points between 1997 (9%) and 2000 (6.3% - still much about Euroland average of 3.9%); a similar effect was observed in Belgium. Thus, the once-and-for-all benefits from monetary integration are distributed asymmetrically in Euroland, where Italian and Belgian citizens/taxpayers recorded special windfall gains. The second effect implies that Euroland will find it easier to absorb interest rate shocks in the future. One should also note that financial market integration in Euroland will lead to a more liquid bond market in which bid-ask spreads are reduced – although not coming close to the US figure for on-the-run issues; in 1997 the US figure was about ½ of the German-French figure for five year maturities (see BIS).

Tab. C10: Deficit-GDP Ratios, Debt-GDP Ratios and Related Figures

General government surplus (+) or deficit (-)					General government gross debt				
	1996	1997	1998	1999		1996	1997	1998	1999
Euro area	**-4,3**	**-2,6**	**-2,0**	**-1,2**	**Euro area**	**75,2**	**74,6**	**73**	**72,2**
Belgium	-3,7	-2,0	-1,0	-0,9	Belgium	128,3	123	117,4	114,4
Germany	-3,4	-2,6	-1,7	-1,2	Germany	59,8	60,9	60,7	61,1
Spain	-5,0	-3,2	-2,6	-1,1	Spain	68	66,7	64,9	63,5
France	-4,2	-3,0	-2,7	-1,8	France	57,1	59	59,3	58,6
Ireland	-0,6	0,8	2,1	2,0	Ireland	74,1	65,3	55,6	52,4
Italy	-7,1	-2,7	-2,8	-1,9	Italy	122,1	119,8	116,3	114,9
Luxemburg	2,7	3,6	3,2	2,4	Luxemburg	6,2	6	6,4	6,2
Netherlands	-1,8	-1,2	-0,8	0,5	Netherlands	75,3	70,3	67	63,8
Austria	-3,8	-1,9	-2,5	-2,0	Austria	68,3	63,9	63,5	64,9
Portugal	-3,8	-2,6	-2,1	-2,0	Portugal	63,6	60,3	56,5	56,8
Finland	-3,2	-1,5	1,3	2,3	Finland	57,1	54,1	49	47,1

Tab. C10: Deficit-GDP Ratios, Debt-GDP Ratios and Related Figures (cont.)

Intrest payments in the EU

	1998	1999	2000	2001
B	7,7	7,5	7,2	6,8
D	3,6	3,5	3,5	3,4
E	4,4	4,0	3,7	3,6
F	3,6	3,4	3,3	3,2
IRL	3,1	2,7	2,3	2,1
I	8,0	6,9	6,3	5,9
L	n.a.	n.a.	n.a.	n.a.
NL	4,9	4,5	4,1	3,7
A	4,1	3,9	3,9	3,9
P	3,6	3,4	3,4	3,4
FIN	3,8	3,2	2,9	2,7
EUR-11	4,7	4,3	4,1	3,9
DK	5,2	4,6	4,2	3,9
EL	8,9	8,7	8,1	7,6
S	5,8	5,3	4,5	3,9
UK	3,6	3,3	3,0	2,8
EU-15	**4,7**	**4,3**	**4,0**	**3,8**

Source: EU Commission (2000) and ECB (2000b) Annual Report

ECB monetary policy has indirectly encouraged creation of an integrated Euroland financial market. From a theoretical perspective the benefits of financial market integration can be summarized by the REBELO endogenous growth model which explains output growth g_Y by the following equation (with Z is capital productivity, θ is an efficiency parameter of the financial system, s is the savings rate and δ the depreciation rate)

$$g_Y = Z\theta\, s - \delta$$

Thus, financial market integration could influence output growth by affecting capital productivity, the efficiency of the financial system or the savings rate (TSURU, 2000).

As stock markets gain a larger role in Euroland – this might indeed be expected as the Euroland's issuing of new stocks exceeded that of the US in the first half of 2000 – one may anticipate impulses for a higher capital productivity. As the Euro intensifies competition in Euroland one also can expect a rise of the efficiency parameter provided that not problems in (fragmented) banking supervision lead to new inefficiency problems in Euroland. However, the savings rate is likely to decrease as strong competition in the banking system reduces equity capital requirements of investors interested in new real estate or industrial projects.

The integration of Euroland financial markets will probably benefit from the growth of the internet since it reduces information and transaction costs on the one hand, and on the other hand, it gives newcomers – e.g. internet service providers – excellent opportunities for market entry. With many firms in Euroland interested in getting access to capital by issuing bonds there should be a boom in the corporate bonds market which can easily be organized on a B2B internet platform.

For Euroland, firms more integrated financial markets mean a new advantage for financing investment at home and abroad. Firms in peripheral countries – which used to have high inflation and high real interest rates – should benefit particularly from the financial market effects of monetary integration. With larger financial markets emerging in Europe, the minimum optimum banking scale has increased and thus larger banks are likely to be created. With respect to allocation and competition it should make a large difference whether external growth of banks is mainly achieved via national mergers – effectively reducing competition – or via international mergers on a European scale which would raise competition.

The Euro, Unemployment and Globalization

While the Euro and the ESCB have started with a favorable low inflation rate, there is some concern about high unemployment rates in Euroland which could benefit from a global economic upswing in 2000/2001. If high unemployment persists in EU core countries the next downswing could create major political conflicts.

With the creation of a more transparent market in Euroland there are strong incentives to rationalize production – including via international mergers and acquisitions - which will partly imply international relocation of production; to the extent that this is associated with intra-Euroland relocation there is only a modest problem for Euroland, but clearly there could be major problems for some high wage countries such as Germany, the Netherlands, France or Belgium where producers of standardized products are very likely to increasingly explore cheaper production in southern countries (e.g. Spain or Portugal). If production is relocated on a larger geographical scale – e.g. with production relocated to Eastern Europe – there could be temporary problems for Euroland. Interestingly, it is the periphery of Euroland which is making the largest progress in terms of reducing unemployment and employment creation, respectively. There are, however, some medium term opportunities for catching-up for Germany, France and Italy if these countries adopt adequate policy reforms and actively exploit the new opportunities of the Internet and the "new economy", respectively. In the US the Internet accounted for about 2.6 million jobs in 1999 and was the fastest growing sector. With the exceptions of Scandinavia and the UK, the EU member countries have been rather slow in picking up the Internet both as a business-to-business platform and as a new technology used by private households for shopping, banking, leisure and learning.

The transatlantic US lead in terms of economic growth in the second half of the 1990s was partly related to its lead in computer usage and Internet dynamics. Facing a very low unemployment rate in 2000/2001 there will be strong motivation for US firms to actively exploit the internet and to thus raise productivity and value-added. This might contribute to a sustained US lead in economic growth as Euroland already faces increased real interest rates in mid-2000 and will hardly benefit from continued real devaluation of the Euro. A typical monetary conditions index – which includes real interest and effective real exchange rate developments – will indicate an expansionary policy course in 1999/2000, but much less so in 2001/2002.

Unemployment problems in Europe have been discussed by various authors who have emphasized lack of regional mobility, insufficient wage differentials across skills and sectors as well as excessive wage pressure (e.g. DECRESSIN/FATAS (1995), SIEBERT (1997), NICKELL (1997), SOSKICE, (1994)).

Regarding unemployment in Euroland and the US, one has to distinguish between divergent transatlantic employment rates and the unemployment phenomenon as such. Euroland's main problem is a lack of new jobs and excessive wage pressure which stimulates rationalization investment. However, not only does Euroland have a problem in the sense that trade unions and employer organizations have pursued a strategy of eliminating older workers' jobs by forcing early retirement – the trade unions hope that this will open up jobs for younger unemployed –, there is also a problem of inefficient investment financed from cash flows (MUELLER/YURTOGLU, 2000) in Germany and other Euroland countries which implies that there is some overemployment. If investment decisions followed capital and stock market logic more closely– as in the US, the UK and in Scandinavian countries – many firms would have lower investment; namely, those with over-ambitious managers who overemphasize growth of the firm. However, as higher dividends are paid out be firms facing a stricter capital market discipline other firms might find it easier to finance higher investments.

While there is considerable structural unemployment - probably as much as 2/3 of overall EU unemployment and a high share of long term unemployed (roughly 50% of overall unemployment where it is only 1/10 in the US) - in Euroland the main problem of Western Europe is insufficient new job growth. This is amply borne out by the fact that the participation ratio in the US strongly increased in the 1980s and 1990s: it reached about 74% in 1998/99. In Euroland, by contrast, the participation ratio stagnated and reached only 58.1% in 1997; Japan recorded 69.5%. Since job growth in OECD countries is mainly related to the creation and growth of new firms, one has to address EU capital market problems if one is to seriously analyze the nature of the employment problem in continental EU countries.

Employment accounted for 64.4% of the total working age population in the Euro area in 1960 which was 3.6 percentage points above the US level. While the employment ratio has continuously increased in the US – with some acceleration after 1984 – and reached 74.6% in 1999, the employment rate in the Euro area fell to 59.4% in 1999 (ECB, 2000). In 1960 the unemployment rate in the Euro area was only 1.4%, but it strongly increased after 1975 – while it remained under the US figure until 1984. In 1999 only 3.3% of the working age population was unemployed which was much below the peak of 7% in 1983. Based on disaggregated employment rates by age for the Euro area the picture is clear: In the period 1984-1999 there was an increase for prime-age workers (aged 30-59) and a decline for the young (15-29) and the old (over 60 years). While the US recorded employment rates of 16% for the male population above 65 and some 8% for the female population the share of people working above 65 in Euroland is very low. This contributes to the financing problems of the pay-as-you-go retirement systems in continental EU countries (only the Netherlands has a more diversified system). As EU firms face high non-wage costs, including rising pension contribution rates in a period of rising life expectancy and a rising ratio of pensioners to workers, this impairs the prospects for employment growth. It is clear that social security reforms in Euroland are urgent (ADDISON/WELFENS, 1998).

In comparing the US and Euroland one will find more labor rigidities in the Old World than in the New World. By labor rigidities we mean e.g. relatively high and long-lasting unemployment compensation and generous redundancy payments and advance notice rules for workers to be laid off. There are, however, considerable differences across Euro countries.

An interesting aspect in diverging transatlantic employment developments concerns the different sectoral distribution of employees. The US share in manufacturing was 14.3% in 1999, while the figure for Euroland was 23.8%. This hardly is an indicator that Euroland's manufacturing industry is almost twice as large as that of the US; rather one may assume that US manufacturing firms are relatively advanced in the outsourcing of services. Indeed, real estate and business services in the US have accounted for 10.9% of jobs in 1999, while Euroland reached only 7.3%. Moreover, the US figure for wholesale, retail trade and repairs was 23.5%, while that for Euroland was only 13.3% (ECB, 2000). At the same time one may note that Euroland probably still had some hidden unemployment: The share of jobs in transport and communications was 6.2% while that in the US was only 4.6%. Further privatization, deregulation and restructuring in Euroland in this sector is likely to lead to job losses and to cost reductions. This is not necessarily a net loss of jobs since transport and communication services are largely inputs for all other industries which should expand as input prices of transport and telecommunication services fall.

According to ECB figures the Euro area has a high share of older workers who will be retiring early. While the standard age for retirement is 65 in most EU countries inactivity rates for male workers aged 55-64 increased from 42% in 1983 to 51% in 1999. By contrast, the US figure increased only slightly – by 2 percentage points – and stood at about 32% in 1999.

Another problem in the Euro zone is the large regional dispersion of unemployment. In 1988 the gap between regional unemployment rates in Italy and Spain exceeded 20 percentage points, in Germany 18, in France nearly 16; but the latter showed a lower standard deviation than the other three countries. All this points to insufficient regional wage differentiation on the one hand, on the other hand to insufficient differentiation in unemployment compensation. With regards to the latter, one might indeed consider basing unemployment compensation partly on the regional unemployment rates, which would raise the pressure in high unemployment regions to search for a new job – within the region, and outside. It would also be useful to encourage job searching and employment by a premium which government could pay to those who accept a new job and keep it at least for one year.

Structural Change, Adjustment and Employment

From a theoretical perspective one can analyze the effects of integration on labor markets in several ways where the starting point is the reduction of transaction costs in the tradables sector – in the case of trade integration – and in the overall economy, respectively (monetary integration):

- Macroeconomic approach, e.g. with a focus on the link between wealth effects of monetary integration and the implied adjustments in all macro markets; (think of the CA surplus phenomenon in the context of monetary approach to the balance of payments).
- Structural adjustment model whose focus is on the structural changes associated with monetary integration, e.g. to which extent monetary union will stimulate the expansion of sectors which are skill-intensive on the one hand, and, on the other hand the contraction of sectors.
- Intergenerational approach with emphasis on the dynamic wealth and income effects within a multi-period model.
- Microeconomic analysis with the main focus on the impact of monetary union on individual household behavior.

Skills, Technological Specialization and Unemployment in an Open Economy

Economic globalization has raised the global offering of unskilled labor where major developments concern the economic opening up of China in the 1980s and – less dramatically – that of Eastern Europe and Russia in the 1990s. China's continuing rural labor excess supply and the population growth in other developing countries is equivalent to a continuous increase in global unskilled labor supply. Consequently, the relative wage position of unskilled workers in OECD countries has eroded in countries with a flexible wage setting (US) or the relative unemployment rates of unskilled workers have strongly increased – as in Germany and the EU, respectively. Downward wage pressure on unskilled labor stems from trade, i.e. rising exports of labor-intensive products from developing countries, but also from outward OECD FDI flows in sectors which are intensive in unskilled labor; one may assume that such FDI flows mainly go to developing countries, newly industrializing countries and post-socialist Eastern Europe so that labor productivity in these countries will gradually increase; real wages will follow in the long term.

The case of (West-) Germany clearly shows that sectors which are skill-intensive strongly create new jobs while those employing mainly unskilled personnel suffered from net job destruction (LICHTBLAU, 1998).

In (West-) Germany the unemployment rate for highly skilled personnel hovered between 0.5 and 4 % in the period 1983-95 while that rate for medium skilled workers and employees was relatively higher, namely by about 2 percentage points. The unemployment rate for unskilled workers rose strongly after 1972 – the last year of full employment in Germany – and its level was about twice as high as that of medium skilled personnel.

EU eastern expansion lets one expect that unskilled workers in the EU-15 group will suffer from the new all-European economic specialization. However, there are some caveats related to the role of trading costs and their reduction, respectively: E.g. in Austria the chemical industry and textiles employ relatively much unskilled labor but the net effect of eastern expansion is shown to be positive (KEUSCHNIGG/KOHLER, 1998); the Keuschnigg-Kohler computable general equilibrium model shows that the removal of initially relatively high sectoral trading costs lead to such a strong demand expansion that the Austrian textiles and chemicals sector can actually expand their net exports. For some Austrian firms such a development might indeed be further facilitated by cheaper intermediate imports from Eastern Europe which allow to profitably expand exports to third country markets.

EMU, Labor Market Rigidities and Unemployment

Taking a look at labor market characteristics of EU countries one can find large differences. Participation ratios vary between 50 % (Italy and Spain) to about 70% in Portugal and Scandinavia; there are also considerable differences in terms of the unemployment rate and the unemployment duration across EU countries. Some of these distinct developments might be linked to different degrees of labor market rigidities, namely the level of the unemployment benefits (e.g. 26% of the average pay for ½ year in Italy, one to three years in Germany and 73% of the average pay for 30 months in Denmark) and the unemployment duration, differences in skills and skill upgrading. From a theoretical point of view a high level of labor market rigidities tends to raise the unemployment rate.

In the model of MEHREZ and VALLA (1998) which is based on monopolistic competition and trade in a two country model with labor market rigidities it can be shown that the equilibrium unemployment rate in country I is positively related to labor market rigidities in country II. From this perspective Germany has an interest that its Euroland partners reduce the level of rigidities, at the same time France and other Euroland countries have an interest that Germany reduce its labor market rigidities. It is unclear whether there is an incentive compatible EU political regime which encourages politicians to pursue labor market deregulation at home and to call for such measures abroad.

Two-Sector Approach to Full Employment

The MEHREZ/VALLA (1998) model is an ad-hoc specification of the labor market in the sense that higher unemployment rates lead to lower real wages. While there is no consistent justification given by the authors, one can, however, develop such a link in a quasi-neoclassical framework. Assume that there are two sectors, the consumption sector and the capital equipment sector. If we assume for simplicity that labor supply in the capital goods sector is inelastic, a wage level above the equilibrium level $\underline{w_1}$ will lead to a lower real wage income than at full employment. We assume that demand for consumption goods is proportionate to labor income of the two sectors ($w1L1 + w2L2=C^d$). Under such a quasi-classical assumption excessive wages in sector 1 and generous unemployment compensation will reduce overall labor income and thus go along with quasi-neoclassical unemployment. It is neoclassical in the sense that lower real wages in the capital goods sector would lead to higher employment in the consumption goods sector, and it is Keynesian in the sense that the reduction of employment in the consumption goods sector goes along with a decline in consumption demand and aggregate demand, respectively.

Globalization and Eastern EU Expansion

The EU is facing a first wave of EU eastern expansion right after the planned introduction of Euro cash in 2002. It is important to understand what will be the impact of trade liberalization in Europe and the whole world. Indeed, there will be both rising global trade and foreign direct investment – coming under the heading of economic globalization – in the future.

Trade has a direct effect on growth, but it might also have important effects on the choice of technology and thereby be more important than the direct effects would suggest. Clearly, exports facilitate exploitation of scale economies and imports support economic catching-up by giving the country access to high quality intermediate imports, but also by exposing the import-competing firms to the pressure from the world market. Moreover, with rising per capita income there will be more intra-industry trade, which in turn is partly related to vertical intra-industry trade which means trading in products of different qualities.

While neoclassical theory suggest that economic opening up will lead to international convergence of factor price ratios and of absolute factor rewards reality often has shown – at least temporarily – that international income differentials have increased and that income differentials within the country that opened up have increased.

Recent analysis (survey: JANSEN, 2000) has shed light on the issue of wage dispersion in the sense of the wage ratio of skilled to that of unskilled labor. MANASSE/TURRINI (1999) focus on a model with intra-industry trade, including vertical intra-industry trade which means trading of different product qualities. The model assumes that in order to export, firms have to pay some fixed costs. As the country opens up for trade those companies producing the high qualities can afford to pay the fixed cost. Thus, only the high skilled workers employed in the production of high quality products will benefit from trade. Intra-industry trade thus could lead to increasing wage inequality. This is, of course, not an argument against trade; rather it points to the need of training and retraining plus some redistributive activities of government aiming at maintaining a minimum social cohesion.

DURANTON (1999) emphasizes in his model the role of intermediate products which can be of low or of high quality, but only skilled workers are able to produce the high quality intermediate products. As final goods producers decide whether to use advanced technology or low technology which is inferior in productivity the decision in favor of advanced technology could strongly benefit skilled workers. It is possible that in autarchy advanced technology is not used because of a lack of high quality intermediates due to the scarcity of skilled labor. With economic opening up high quality intermediates can be imported and high skilled workers will improve their relative wage as they will no longer work in the production of low quality goods.

A third mechanism was pointed out by GROSSMAN (1999) who presented a model with two different sectors: One sector in which workers are paid according to their individual marginal product (e.g. the software industry) while the other sector technically cannot distinguish individual marginal products and therefore pays according to the average worker's talent in this sector (e.g. automotive industry). In this setting we will see the most talented workers being active in the software industry. When two countries with different distributions of workforce start trading we will observe that in the country with the more heterogeneous workforce more people will be working in the software sector. When the two countries start trading the country with the more heterogeneous workforce will specialize in software and export software products, while the other country will export cars. This tends to increase the inequality in the „software country" while the opposite holds true for the country with the more homogenous workforce.

Taking into account a macroeconomic production function and adopting a growth perspective it holds that overall economic growth (with g denoting a growth rate) can be written as

$$gY = b1gL + b2gN + b3gK + b4gT - b5Z$$

where L is unskilled labor, N is skilled labor, K the stock of capital and T the rate of technological progress which itself is influenced by various variables, including government R&D support, the trade volume and foreign direct investment inflows. Z is the degree of political instability which negatively affects growth. KORMENDI/MCGUIRE have focussed on a broader set of variables to explain growth in a cross-country regression.

References

ADDISON, J. and WELFENS, P.J.J., eds. (1998), Labor Markets and Social Security, Heidelberg and New York: Springer.

ASEA, P.K. and MENDOZA, E.G. (1994), Do Long-Run Productivity Differentials Explain Long-Run Exchange Rates?, IMF Working Paper, WP/94/60, Washington, DC.

BÉNASSY-QUÉRÉ, A. and MOJON, B. (1998), EMU and Transatlantic Exchange-Rate Stability, Paper presented at Deutsch-Französisches Wirtschaftspolitisches Forum, "The EMU's Exchange Rate Policy," 12-13 January 1998, ZEI, Bonn.

BILSON, J.F.O. (1979), Recent Developments in Monetary Models of Exchange Rate Determination, IMF Staff Papers 26, 201-223.

BIS (1998), 68th Annual Report, Basle, see www.bis.org.

BLACK, S. (1997), The Relation Between the Core and the Periphery in Monetary Union, paper prepared for the Conference "Real Exchange Rates and European Monetary Union", Mainz, May 22-23, 1997, mimeo.

BOFINGER, P. (1994), Is Europe an Optimum Currency Area?, in STEINHERR, A., ed., 30 Years of European Monetary Integration: From the Werner Plan to EMU, London: Longman.

BOHN, F. (2000), Monetary Union and Fiscal Stability, Heidelberg and New York: Springer.

BORCHERT, M. (1998), Design-Probleme einer einheitlichen Geldpolitik in Europa, in: List Forum für Wirtschafts- und Finanzpolitik, 24, 37-56.

BRETSCHGER, L. (1998), Wachstumstheorie, 2nd edition, München: Oldenbourg.

BROOKES, M. (1998), The Arrival of the Euro, Goldman, Sachs & Co., Frankfurt/M, mimeo.

CALMFORS, L. (1997), Unemployment, Labour-Market Reform and EMU, Institute for International Economic Studies.

CHIANG, A.C. (1984), Fundamental Methods of Mathematical Economics, 3rd edition, New York: McGraw-Hill.

CLAUSEN, V. (2000), Asummetric Monetary Transmission in Europe, Heidelberg and New York: Springer.

CORDEN, W.M. (1993), Economic Policy, Exchange Rates and the International System, Oxford: Oxforder University Press.

CORNEO, G. (1995), National Wage Bargaining in an Internationally Integrated Product Market, European Journal of Political Economy, 11, 503-520.

DANTHINE, J.-P. and HUNT, J. (1994), Wage Bargaining Structure, Employment and Economic Integration, Economic Journal, Vol. 104, 528-541.

DARBY, M.R., LIU, Q. and ZUCKER, L.G. (1999), Stakes and Stars: The Effect of Intellectual Human Capital on the Level and Variability of High-Tech Firms´ Market Values, NBER Working Paper, No. 7201, Cambridge, Ma.

DE GRAUWE, P. (1994), The Economics of Monetary Integration, 2nd ed., Oxford: Oxford University Press.

DE MENIL, G. (1999), Real Capital Market Integration in the EU: How Far Has It Gone? What will the Effect of the Euro Be?, Economic Policy, 28, 167-201.

DECRESSIN, J. and FATAS, A. (1995), Regional Labor Market Dynamics in Europe, European Economic Review, Vol. 39, 1627-1655.

DESMET, D.; FRANCIS, T.; HU, A.; KOLLER, T.M. and RIEDEL, G.A. (2000), Valueing dot-coms, The McKinsey Quarterly, 2000, No. 1, McKinsey & Company.

DEUTSCHE BUNDESBANK (1998), Monthly Report, April, No. 4, Frankfurt/M.

DORNBUSCH, R. (1976), Expectations and Exchange Rate Dynamics, Journal of Political Economy, 84, 1167-1176.

DRESDNER BANK, research memo, London

DURANTON, G. (1999), The Futue of the High-Skill Equilibrium in Germany, Oxford Review of Economic Policy, Vol. 15, No. 1, 43-59.

ECB (2000), ECB Monthly Bulletin, May 2000.

ECB (2000b), Annual Report, Frankfurt/M.

EICHENGREEN, B. (1993), Labor Markets and European Monetary Unification, in: MASSON, P. and TAYLOR, M., eds., Policy Issues in the Operation of Currency Unions, Cambridge: Cambridge University Press, 130-162.

EUROPEAN COMMISSION (1997a), The First Action Plan for Innovation in Europe, Brussels; document drawn up on the basis of COM(96) 589 final.

EUROPEAN COMMISSION (1997b), External Aspects of Economic and Monetary Union, Euro Papers 1, Brussels.

EUROPEAN COMMISSION (2000), The EU Economy: 1999 review, Belgium.

FAMA, E. (1991), Efficient Capital Markets: II, Journal of Finance, Vol. 46, 1575-1617.

FRANKEL, J.A. and ROSE, A.K. (1996), The Endogeneity of the Optimum Currency Area Criteria, NBER Working Paper 5700.

FRATIANNI, M. and VON HAGEN, J. (1992), The EMS and European Monetary Union, Boulder, Co.: Westview.

FROOT, K.A., STEIN, J.C. (1991), Exchange Rates and Foreign Direct Investment: An Imperfect Capital Markets Approach, Quarterly Journal of Economics, November, 1191-1217.

GÄRTNER, M. (1993), Macroeconomics Under Flexible Exchange Rates, New York et al.: Harvester Wheatsheaf.

GÄRTNER, M. (1997), Makroökonomik flexibler und fester Wechselkurse, 2nd ed., Heidelberg.

GENSER, B., HAUFLER, A., HETTICH, F. and SCHMIDT, C. (1998), International Taxation and Pollution Control: How Should Priorities be Chosen in the European Union's Tax Policy Agenda, paper presented at the symposium International Arrangements for Global Economic Integration, University of Konstanz, February 26-28.

GOTTSCHALK, P. (1997), Inequality, Income Growth and Mobility: The Basic Facts, Journal of Economic Perspectives 11, 21-40.

GROS, D. and HEFEKER, C. (1998), Factor Mobility, European Integration and Unemployment, Brussels, mimeo.

GROSSMAN, G., HELPMAN, E. (1991), Innovation and Growth in the Global Economy, MIT Press, Cambridge: MA.

GROSSMAN, G.M. (1999), Imperfect Labour Contracts and International Trade, CEPR Discussion Paper 2240, London.

GRÜNER, H.P. and HEFEKER, C. (1998), How Will EMU Affect Unemployment and Inflation, Scandinavian Journal of Economics, forthcoming.

HALL, B.H. (1999), Innovation and Market Value, NBER Working Paper No. 6984.

HEFEKER, C. (1995), Monetary Union or Currency Competition? Currency Arrangements for Monetary Stability in East and West, Constitutional Political Economy, Vol. 6, 57-69.

IMF (1997), International Capital Markets, Washington, DC.

IWD (1998), Viel Staat und noch mehr Diener, in: IWD - Informationsdienst des Instituts der deutschen Wirtschaft, Cologne.

JANSEN, M. (2000), International Trade and the Position of European Low-skilled Labour, in: ADDISON, J. and WELFENS, P.J.J. (eds.), Labor Markets and Social Security, 2nd revised and enlarged edition, Heidelberg and New York: Springer (forthcoming).

JOHNSON, K.H. (1994), International Dimensions of European Monetary Union: Implications for the Dollar, International Finance Discussion Paper No. 496, Washington, DC, Board of Governors of the Federal Reserve System.

JUNGMITTAG, A. (2000), Internationale Innovationsdynamik und Spezialisierungsstruktur: Empirische Befunde und wirtschaftspolitische Implikationen, Beitrag zum EIIW-Workshop Wachstums- und Innovationspolitik in Deutschland und Europa, 14.04.2000, Potsdam.

KENEN, P.B. (1995), Capital Controls, the EMS and EMU, Economic Journal, Vol. 105, 181-192.

KENEN, P.B. (1998), EMU and Transatlantic Economic Relations, paper presented at the 5th HWWA Conference on "Transatlantic Relations in a Global Economy," May 6-8, 1998, HWWA Discussion Paper No. 60, Hamburg.

KEUSCHNIGG, C. and KOHLER, W. (1997), Eastern Enlargement of the EU: How Much Is It Worth for Austria, Discussion Paper No. 9723, University of Linz.

KRAVIS, I.B. and LIPSEY, R.E. (1983), Towards an Explanation of National Price Levels, Princeton Studies in International Finance, No. 52, Princeton, N.J.

KRAVIS, I.B. and LIPSEY, R.E. (1987), The Assessment of National Price Levels, in: ARNDT, S.W. and RICHARDSON, J.D., eds., Real Financial Linkages among Open Economies, Cambridge MA.

KRAY, A. (1998), In Search of the Macroeconomic Effects of Capital Account Liberalization, Washington DC: The World Bank.

LANE, T. et al. (1999), IMF Supporte Programs in Indonesia, Korea and Thailand: A Preliminary Assessment, IMF Occasional Paper No. 178, Washington DC.

LICHTBLAU, K. (1998), Beschäftigungsentwicklung, Strukturwandel und Qualifikationspotential des Humankapitals, IW-Trends, 2/98.

MANASSE, P. and TURRINI, A. (1999), Tade, Wages and Superstars, CEPR Discussion Paper 2262.

McCAULEY, R.N. (1997), The Euro and the Dollar, Essays in International Finance 205, Princeton: International Finance Section, Princeton University.

MEHREZ, G. and N. VALLA (1998), EMU: What if the Shocks are in the Labor Markets?, Georgetown University and European University Institute, Florence.

MEYER, B., WELFENS, P.J.J. (1999), Innovation-Augmented Ecological Tax Reform: Theory, Model Simulation and New Policy Implications, EIIW Discussion Paper No. 65, September.

MUELLER, D.C.; YURTOGLU, B.B. (2000), Country Legal Environments and Corporate Investment Performance, German Economic Review, Vol. 1, 187-220.

MUNDELL, R.A. (1993), EMU and the International Monetary System, in: GIOVANNINI A. et al., eds., The Monetary Future of Europe, London: Centre for Economic Policy Research.

NICKELL, S. (1997), Unemployment and Labor Market Rigidities: Europe versus North America, Journal of Economic Perspectives, Summer, 55-74.

OBSTFELD, M., ROGOFF, D. (1996), Foundations of International Macroeconomics, Cambridge Mass.: MIT Press.

RICHARDS, A.J. and TERSMAN, G.H.R. (1996), Growth, Nontradables and Price Convergence in the Baltics, Journal of Comparative Economics, 23, 121-145.

ROMER, P.M. (1990), Endogenous Technical Change, Journal of Political Economy, 1990, S71-S102.

ROTHER, P.C. (1997), Geldnachfragetheoretische Implikationen der Europäischen Währungsunion, Heidelberg: Physica/Springer.

SAINT-PAUL, G. (1996), The Rise and Persistence of Rigidities, CEPR Discussion Paper No. 1571, London.

SIEBERT, H. (1996), ed., Monetary Policy in an Integrated World, Tübingen: Mohr.

SIEBERT, H. (1997), Labour Market Rigidities: At the Root of Unemployment in Europe, Journal of Economic Perspectives, Summer, 37-54.

SOSKICE, D. (1994), Labour Markets in the EC in the 1990's, Social Europe, Supplement #1, European Commission, 61-73.

SVR (1998); German Council of Economic Advisers, Jahresgutachten 1998/99, Bonn.

TAVLAS, G. (1993), The "New" Theory of Optimum Currency Areas, The World Economy, No. 16, 664-685.

TILLY, R. and WELFENS, P.J.J., eds., (1996), European Economic Integration as a Challenge to Industry and Government, Heidelberg and New York.

TOBIN, J. (1958), Liquidity Preference as Behavior Towards Risk, in: Review of Economic Studies, 25, 65-86.

TOBIN, J. (1961), Money, Capital and Other Stores of Value, in: The American Economic Review, 51, 26-37.

TOBIN, J. (1965), Money and Economic Growth, Econometrica 1965, 671-684.

TSURU (2000), Finance and Growth, OECD, Paris, forthcoming.

TURNOVSKY, O. (1997), International Macroeconomic Dynamics, Cambridge Mass.: MIT Press.

UNCTAD (1993), Explaining and Forecasting Regional Flows of Foreign Direct Investment, Geneva.

WELFENS, P.J.J. (1992), Market-oriented Systemic Transformations in Eastern Europe, Heidelberg and New York: Springer.

WELFENS, P.J.J. (1998a), Labor Costs, Unemployment and Innovation, Discussion Paper No. 43, European Institute for International Economic Relations, Potsdam.

WELFENS, P.J.J. (1998b), Trade and Optimum Tariffs: A Note in the Context of Foreign Direct Investment, EIIW Working Paper No. 48, European Institute of International Economic Relations at the University of Potsdam, June.

WELFENS, P.J.J. (1999a), Globalization of the Economy, Unemployment and Innovation, Heidelberg and New York: Springer.

WELFENS, P.J.J. (1999b), The Start of the Euro, International Monetary Relations and Inflation, EIIW Discussion Paper No. 62, Potsdam.

WELFENS, P.J.J. (2000), Modern Exchange Rate Theory and Schumpetrian Economic Analysis: New Approach and Application to the Euro, EIIW Discussion Paper No. 77, Potsdam.

WELFENS, P.J.J. and WOLF, H., eds., (1997), Banking, International Capital Markets and Growth in Europe, Heidelberg and New York.

WELFENS, P.J.J., AUDRETSCH, D., ADDISON, J. and GRUPP, H. (1998), Technological Competition, Employment and Innovation Policy in OECD Countries, Heidelberg and New York: Springer.

WELFENS, P.J.J., ed. (1996), European Monetary Integration, 3rd revised and enlarged edition, Heidelberg and New York: Springer.

WELFENS, P.J.J., ed. (1997a), European Monetary Union, Heidelberg and New York: Springer.

WELFENS, P.J.J., ed. (1997b), Economic Aspects of German Unification, 2nd edition, Heidelberg and New York: Springer.

WELFENS, P.J.J., EICHHORN, B., PALINKAS, P. (1998), Euro – neues Geld für Europa, Frankfurt/M.: Campus.

WELFENS, P.J.J., JUNGMITTAG, A. (1997), Political Economy of EMU Stabilization Policy, in: WELFENS (ed.), European Monetary Union, Heidelberg and New York: Springer.

WILLIAMSON, J. and MILLER, M.M. (1987), Targets and Indicators: A Blueprint for the International Coordination of Economic Policies, Washington, DC: Institute for International Economics.

List of Figures

List of Tables

Further Publications by *Paul J. J. Welfens*

P. J. J. Welfens
Market-oriented Systemic Transformations in Eastern Europe
Problems, Theoretical Issues, and Policy Options
1992. XII, 261 pp. 20 figs., 29 tabs.,
Hardcover, ISBN 3-540-55793-8

M. W. Klein, P. J. J. Welfens
Multinationals in the New Europe and Global Trade
1992. XV, 281 pp. 24 figs., 75 tabs.,
Hardcover, ISBN 3-540-54634-0

R. Tilly, P. J. J. Welfens
European Economic Integration as a Challenge to Industry and Government
Contemporary and Historical Perspectives on International Economic Dynamics
1996. X, 558 pp. 43 figs., Hardcover,
ISBN 3-540-60431-6

P. J. J. Welfens
European Monetary Integration
EMS Developments and International Post-Maastricht Perspectives
3rd revised and enlarged edition
1996. XVIII, 384 pp. 14 figs., 26 tabs.,
Hardcover, ISBN 3-540-60260-7

P. J. J. Welfens
European Monetary Union
Transition, International Impact and Policy Options
1997. X, 467 pp. 50 figs., 31 tabs.,
Hardcover, ISBN 3-540-63309-7

P. J. J. Welfens, G. Yarrow
Telecommunications and Energy in Systemic Transformation
International Dynamics, Deregulation and Adjustment in Network Industries
1997. XII, 501 pp. 39 figs., Hardcover,
ISBN 3-540-61586-5

P. J. J. Welfens, H. C. Wolf
Banking, International Capital Flows and Growth in Europe
Financial Markets, Savings and Monetary Integration in a World with Uncertain Convergence
1997. XIV, 458 pp. 22 figs., 63 tabs.,
Hardcover, ISBN 3-540-63192-5

P. J. J. Welfens
Economic Aspects of German Unification
Expectations, Transition Dynamics and International Perspectives
2nd revised and enlarged edition
1996. XV, 527 pp. 34 figs., 110 tabs.,
Hardcover, ISBN 3-540-60261-5

P. J. J. Welfens, D. Audretsch,
J. T. Addison and H. Grupp
Technological Competition, Employment and Innovation Policies in OECD Countries
1998. VI, 231 pp. 16 figs., 20 tabs.,
Hardcover, ISBN 3-540-63439-8

J. T. Addison, P. J. J. Welfens
Labor Markets and Social Security
Wage Costs, Social Security Financing and Labor Market Reforms in Europe
1998. IX, 404 pp. 39 figs., 40 tabs.,
Hardcover, ISBN 3-540-63784-2

P. J. J. Welfens
EU Eastern Enlargement and the Russian Transformation Crisis
1999. X, 151 pp. 12 figs., 25 tabs., Hardcover,
ISBN 3-540-65862-9

P. J. J. Welfens
Globalization of the Economy, Unemployment and Innovation
1999. VI, 255 pp. 11 figs., 31 tabs.,
Hardcover, ISBN 3-540-65250-7

P. J. J. Welfens, G. Yarrow, R. Grinberg,
C. Graack
Towards Competition in Network Industries
Telecommunications, Energy and Transportation in Europe and Russia
1999. XXII, 570 pp. 63 figs., 63 tabs.,
Hardcover, ISBN 3-540-65859-9

P. J. J. Welfens, J. T. Addison,
D. B. Audretsch, T. Gries, H. Grupp
Globalization, Economic Growth and Innovation Dynamics
1999. X, 160 pp. 15 figs., 15 tabs.,
Hardcover, ISBN 3-540-65858-0

R. Tilly, P. J. J. Welfens
Economic Globalization, International Organizations and Crisis Management
Contemporary and Historical Perspectives on Growth, Impact and Evolution of Major Organizations in an Interdependent World
2000. XII, 408 pp. 11 figs., 20 tabs.,
Hardcover, ISBN 3-540-65863-7

P. J. J. Welfens, E. Gavrilenkov
Restructuring, Stabilizing and Modernizing the New Russia
Economic and Institutional Issues
2000. XIV, 516 pp. 82 figs., 70 tabs.,
Hardcover, ISBN 3-540-67429-2

P. J. J. Welfens
European Monetary Union and Exchange Rate Dynamics
New Approaches and Applications to the Euro
2001. X, 159 pp. 26 figs., 12 tabs.,
Hardcover, ISBN 3-540-67914-6

MIX
Papier aus verantwortungsvollen Quellen
Paper from responsible sources
FSC® C105338

If you have any concerns about our products,
you can contact us on
ProductSafety@springernature.com

In case Publisher is established outside the EU,
the EU authorized representative is:
Springer Nature Customer Service Center GmbH
Europaplatz 3, 69115 Heidelberg, Germany

Printed by Libri Plureos GmbH
in Hamburg, Germany